Finding Profitable Stocks

Screens & Strategies

Tony Pow

Why you invest

You need to learn about investing sooner or later in your life. You need to take some calculated risks. Compare the returns of the following assets: cash, CDs, treasury bills, bonds, real estate and stocks. We start with the risk-free investments and end with the riskiest. It turns out that the average returns are in the opposite order. Cash and CDs are not risk-free as inflation eats our profits. For example, the real return is negative for the 2% return in a CD and a 3% inflation rate. In addition you have to pay taxes for the 'returns'. <u>Our capitalist system punishes us for not taking risk</u>.

There are two kinds of risk: blind risk and calculated risk. If you buy a stock due to a recommendation from a commentator on TV or a tip, most likely you are taking a blind risk. It would be the same in buying a house without thoroughly evaluating the house and its neighborhood. When you buy stocks with a proven strategy (i.e. when/what stocks to buy and when/what stocks to sell), you are taking a calculated risk. In the long run, stocks with calculated and educated risks are profitable.

Be a turtle investor by investing in value stocks and holding for longer time periods (a year or more). "Buy and Monitor" is better an approach than "Buy and Hold" as some could lose all the stock values such as in the failure of Enron.

For experienced investors, shorting, short-term trading and covered calls would make you good profits. Simple market timing would reduce your losses during market down turns. If you buy a market ETF and use my simple market timing, you should have beaten the market by a wide margin from 2000 to 2019.

With so many frauds and poor management, do not trust anyone with your investing. Do not buy investing instruments that are highly marketed such as annuity and term insurance.

If you are a handy man and do not mind to satisfy the constant requests of your tenants, buy real estate in growing areas could be very profitable in the long run. Take advantage of the tax laws such as investing in a 401K especially the part that is matched by your company and/or a Roth IRA.

Why you want to read this book

It should improve your financial health substantially. There are about a million investment books. Why we need another one?

- I select proven ideas from more than 100 books besides my original ideas and experiences. I also include links to current articles that will bring more depth to the topic. It is not a novel or documenting the story of my life. All related chapters are grouped in a section for easy future reference. Some chapters are not easy to digest as they have a lot of pointers and some may require you to try them out yourself.

- My friend and I were making similar incomes. I retired 10 years earlier than he and I had more than 4 times he had. Following the right screens that have proven recently is a good reason.

- A best seller was written by a young writer whose main income was from his books and none from his investing. His book is good for beginners or you want to brush up your English. Most of my incomes are from investing.

- Many popular books claiming the authors making millions. However, usually their techniques are hard to follow. Many admitted they had been bankrupted many times. Hence, their chance of bankrupting again is very high. Is bankruptcy fine with you? I cannot afford bankruptcy past and present. My techniques minimize risking my money.

- There are many popular books. They worked very well at one time and folks making millions following the advices. However, look at their recent performances of the last five years. Most of them cannot even beat the S&P 500 index.

- Watch out reviews that are written by friends. As of 8/2015 I do not know any of reviewers on my books. Check out my success stories.
- Why you want to invest? Our capitalist system punishes us for not taking risk. To illustrate, 50 years ago you had a choice not to invest your $10,000, invest it in the stock market or buy real estate. Your buying power of your cash is eaten by inflation. Most likely the other choices beat inflation by huge margins.

Contents

Why you invest 2
Why you want to read this book 3
Introduction 6
      Disclaimer 10
Book 1: Simple Techniques 11
      How to start 12
  2   Investing for 'lazy' folks 13
    An example 15
  5   Simplest market timing 16
  6   Rotate four ETFs 20
  8   The best strategy 22
  9   Don'ts for beginners 22
  10   Summary 23
Book 2: Finding Stocks 26
  1   Where the websites are 27
  2   *Finviz.com screener* 30
    A screener example 31
    Other sources 32
    Common parameters 33
    Overview of Finviz.com 39
  3   Sectors to be cautious with 41
  4   GuruFocus 44
  5   Piotroski's F-Score 45
  6   NASDAQ 49
  7   Fidelity 50
  8   ChatGPT (and other AI models) 52
  9   Performance of my screens 55
  10   A scoring system 58
  11   Hedge fund 101 64
Book 3: Evaluating Stocks 70

1	My Performances	71
2	Amazing returns	73
	A scoring system	78

Section I: Fundamental metrics 83

3	Mysteries of P/E	83
	My observations:	88
4	*Fundamental metrics*	92
5	Finviz's parameters	101
	More info from Fidelity	112

Section II: Beyond fundamentals 115

6	Intangibles	115
7	Qualitative analysis	119
8	Manipulators and bankruptcy	121
	Mergers	122
9	Avoid bankrupting companies	126
	An example from a guru on Micron	129

Section III: Selling stocks 131

10	When to sell a stock	131
	Selling a winner	136
11	Examples of overpriced stocks	140
12	Should you hold stocks forever?	141
13	Monitor your traded stocks	144

Section IV: Other sources 145

14	Lessons from a popular book?	145
15	Using Seeking Alpha effectivley	146
16	Making sense of health and investing	146
17	Leveraging Fidelity's Research Tools	147

Bonus: Experiences 150

Section 1: Performance form "Best Stocks" series 151

1	Past Performances	151

Section 2: Gurus' experiences 159

1	Pointers from short-term gurus	159
2	Tips from Peter Lynch	160
3	Charles Munger: 12 common mistakes	162
4	Making 20% return year after year	164
5	From a guru (technical analysis)	165
6	Predictions for 2021	166
7	Disrupting innovation	168

Epilogue 169

Appendix 1 – All my books 170
    Best stocks to buy for 2025 175
    Art of Investing 176

Appendix 2: Reviews by the unbiased AI 180
    Review of "Art of Investing 5th Edition " 9/10 180
        ChatGPT Review 180
        DeepSeek Review 181
    Review of " Best stocks to buy for 2025" 184
    Review of "Sector Rotation 5th Edition" rated 9.5 186
    Review of "Your first dollar for smart investing " 188
        ChatGPT 188
        Final Thoughts from DeepSeek: 189
    Review of "Momentum Investing 3rd Edition " 190
    Review of "Using profitable investment sites" rated 8 .. 191
    Review of "Investing successes and blunders" 192

Appendix 3 - Our window to the investing world 194

Appendix 4 - ETFs / Mutual Funds 194

Appendix 5 - Links 200

Introduction

There are about 4,000 of stocks (about 30,000 if you include smaller stocks and stocks on foreign exchanges). How can you find the winners? Screening stocks can give you a manageable list of candidates worth your further evaluation.

You can use one of the simple screens that are available to you free from many web sites such as Finviz.com and the one from your broker to find a handful of stocks. The filter criteria could be "P/E < 10", "Sales Growth by 20%" or a combination. If the screens consistently find you winners, they are good.

It is more complicated than that. Otherwise there will be no poor folks. However, most screened stocks should be evaluated. Among the 50 or so screens, there is only one evergreen screen that gives consistent stocks that perform. Some screens work better than others in different phases of the market cycle and/or different market conditions such as during the end of year. You need to use different screens for different purposes. For example, stress on value parameters such as "P/E" for value stocks that have to be held for a longer time than momentum stocks. This book is similar to my other book "Art of Investing: Finding Stocks".

How to use this book

Most graphs and tables are in landscape orientation (recommended for small screens) for both paperback and e-readers. Some graphs may not be displayed adequately on a small screen of an e-reader. E-readers may be available in the current version of Windows, so you can read e-books on the larger screen of your PC. For better orientation, just flip the e-readers 90 degrees. Some reader lets you select a table or a graph to display it to fit the screen.

A link is usually included for the most screens. Copy it to your browser to display the graphs on your PC if desirable. Instructions on how to produce some graphs are provided as you should try them out. One example is how to produce a chart on detecting market crashes.

The **font size** (Ctrl Minus for browser implementation of e-readers) and line spacing of most e-book formats can be adjusted. The unknown, special character is the "smiling face" that the current Kindle does not convert correctly as of this writing.

There are clickable links to web articles. Most of them are from my own web sites and public web sites such as Wikipedia. Some public links may not be available in the future as they are not under my control and my book offerings may change.

These links extend the usefulness of this book by making available specific topics that may not be interesting to every reader. It also provides articles (most are not written by me) for more in-depth analyzes.

Fidelity Video provides video clips to explain some basic terms and it may require Fidelity customers to sign on in order to view them. Check the trial offer from Fidelity. YouTube offers similar video lessons.

The current version provides most of the links the paperback readers can enter into your browser. Get the same information by entering a search in Wikipedia such as Dogs of Dow.

'Afterthoughts' includes my additional comments and ideas of minor importance.

There are fillers with tips, refreshing pictures (taken by me) and jokes (most original) to fill up the empty space of the printed book. Fillers, links and afterthoughts may disrupt the flow of reading this book. However, not a single reader so far asks me to take them out even in the digitized version of this book. Many page breaks have been eliminated to improve the flow of the book.

For convenience, this book uses SPY, an Exchange Traded Fund (ETF) simulating the S&P 500, as the benchmark for the market.

Annualized returns (Return * 365 / (Days between)) are used where appropriate for more meaningful comparison. To illustrate, I have a 10% return in 6 months, a 10% in a year and a 10% in 2 years. It is more meaningful to use annualized returns of 20%, 10% and 5% respectively in this example.

Usually I do not include the dividend, so you can add an estimated 1.5% to the annualized return. In addition, compound interest is not used for easier calculation, so the actual return could be even better. Many of my tests are not detailed in this book but their summaries are. It reduces the size of this book that is already huge.

Investopedia and Wikipedia are sources beside Wikipedia to expand some terms and objects described in this book.
http://www.investopedia.com/

There are fillers with tips, refreshing pictures (taken by me) and jokes (most original) to fill up the empty space of the printed book. Fillers, links and afterthoughts may disrupt the flow of reading this book. However, no readers so far ask me to take them out even in the digitized version of this book.

About the author

I graduated from Cal. State University at San Jose in Industrial Engineering and University of Mass. in Amherst with a MS in Industrial Engineering. I have retired from a job in IT. I have been an investor for over 30 years and have written over 20 books on investing. Here is the link to some of my articles I wrote.

Dedication
To all retail investors and future retail investors including my grandchildren.

Acknowledgement

Thanks to all the free sites:
Seeking Alpha, Wikipedia and Investopedia for the many helpful links to enrich this book. Yahoo!Finance and Finviz.com for the tools and charts used in this book.

Important notices
© Tony Pow 2015-2025. Email: pow_tony@yahoo.com.

Version	Paperback	e-book
1.0	07/15	07/15
2.2	12/20	12/20
2.5	09/21	04/25

Printed version. ISBN-13: 978-1514887325 ISBN-10: 1514887320.
No part of this book can be reproduced in any form without the written approval of the author. The original book is Finding Stocks published on 11/13. This is an enhanced version or Version 3 of the original.

Disclaimer

Do not gamble with money that you cannot afford to lose. Past performance is a guideline and is not necessarily indicative of future results. All information is believed to be accurate, but there it is not a guarantee. All the strategies including charts to detect market plunges described have no guarantee that they will make money and they may lose money. Do not trade without doing due diligence and be warned that most data may be obsolete. All my articles and the associated data are for informational and illustration purposes only. I'm not a professional investment counselor or a tax professional. Seek one before you make any investment decisions. The above mentioned also applies for all other advice such as on accounting, taxes, health and any topic mentioned in this book. I am not a professional in any of these fields. Most of the time, I use annualized for a better comparison; 5% in a month is more than 4% in a year for example. For simplicity, most of my returns do not include commissions, exchange fees, order spread and dividends. Same for all the links contained in this book. Some articles may offend some one or some organization unintentionally. If I did, I'm sorry about that. I am politically and religiously neutral. I provide my best efforts to ensure the accuracy of my articles. Data also from different sources was believed to be accurate. However, there is no guarantee that they are accurate and suitable for the current market conditions and /or your individual situations. My publisher and I are not liable for any damages in using this book or its contents.

Book 1: Simple Techniques

For better security, use a two-factor login that should be available in most if not all brokers and most financial institutions such as your banks. To illustrate, after you have logged in, your broker sends a code to your phone to verify you are the rightful owner. Do not be a target of scams by showing your wealth. Do not click unknown web links. Do not lend money and do not give out your credit cards. Do not be greedy. Do not buy the products such as annuities recommended by marketeers, as these products are designed to make big money by them.

An ETF is a basket of stocks. For starters, just trade ETFs such as SPY (an ETF simulating S&P 500 stocks and the market to many), and you can skip the rest of the book. It has been proven, the SPY or VOO has beaten most funds by a good margin. That is why mutual funds are dying.

I prefer VOO which has an expense ratio of 0.03% vs. SPY's 0.09% as of 12/2022). For better diversification, I recommend RSP, an unweighted ETF of the S&P 500 stocks. MDY (0.22%), an ETF for midcap, is also recommended. The last 10 years had been great for SPY until recently. I do not know the next 10 years, and that's why I also recommend MDY together with VOO (or RSP). They represent a wide diversification. Most indexes take out the bad performers and include better additions every year, and hence you do not need to balance your portfolio except for market timing.

It only takes a few minutes every month (more often if the indicators are close to cross over) using the simplest market timing described in Chapter 5. When the market is not plunging, buy or keep SPY (or any ETF that stimulates the market); otherwise sell it. Do the opposite when the market is recovering. The techniques named Death Cross and Golden Cross are the best-kept secrets that have been proven in the last two crashes (2000 and 2008).

The following is from Portfolio Visual (https://www.portfoliovisualizer.com/backtest-portfolio#analysisResults).
From 2000 to Nov., 2022 and including reinvested dividends, the portfolio consisting of 25% SPY, 25% RSP and 50% MDY returns (CAGR) 10% with a max drawdown of 51%.

Do not let the simple techniques that do not require any investing knowledge and time fool you. From 2000 to 2022 (today), it beat the market by a wide margin and I bet it beat most of the fund managers.

If you have less than $50,000 to invest, just buy ETFs. Improve your investing skills by reading investment articles from this book and your broker's website. For example, Fidelity has a lot of information for investors.

Subscription to AAII is recommended. When your portfolio grows more than $50,000, invest on a subscription such as Value Line, GuruFocus, Zacks or IBD (more for momentum traders). Initially, use the information for paper trading on value stocks, which is usually available from brokers.

For the long term, knowledge is most important in your investing life and experience comes next. Retail investors have a lot of advantages over fund managers. However, I advise you NOT to be a trader. Hence, you should ignore the 'fabulous' trade systems that claim to be very profitable. Statistically most amateur traders lose money as they cannot compete with experienced, disciplined traders.

How to start

I recommend trading ETFs first and when the market is not risky. You can skip the following if you do not have time for investing. The very basic terms such as ETF are not fully explained here; try Investopedia for terms you need to know. Otherwise, this book would be doubled in size and it would bore most readers. Investopedia, your broker's website (especially Fidelity) and AAII (requiring subscription) provide many excellent articles. Alternatively, buy a book for beginners.

Here are some freebies:
Click here for Morningstar classroom.
http://morningstar.com/cover/classroom.html
Click here for Vanguard.
https://investor.vanguard.com/investing/investor-education
Click here for Investopedia's Tutorials.
http://www.investopedia.com/university/
Click here for Yahoo!
http://finance.yahoo.com/education/begin_investing
Click here for Fidelity basic in investing.
https://www.fidelity.com/investment-guidance/investing-basics

2 Investing for 'lazy' folks

You have better things to do than investing or you do not have the time, the desire to learn and/or expertise in investing. You should be better off to buy ETFs.

I recommend the following 4 ETFs. If you have $100,000 to invest, buy $25,000 for each recommended ETF. Consult your financial advisor before taking any action. The recommended ETFs should have a large market cap (the ETFs themselves and not the stocks they hold) and have a high volume.

Most returns started on July 1 and ended on July 1 the following year; this article is written on July 20, 2021. All are annualized returns for easy comparison. Fees, commissions and dividends have not been included; you can add the dividend yield and prorate it for YTD return.

Symbol	Name	YTD[1] Return	1 Year[2]	5 Years[3]	Bear[4]
IWF	Russel1000Grow	30%	34%	40%	-33%
QQQ	QQQ	30%	46%	42%	-31%
VTI	Vang. Viper Tot	34%	22%	42%	-35%
VUG	Vang. Growth	37%	33%	41%	-32%
Avg.		31%	34%	41%	-33%
SPY[5]		34%	21%	39%	-35%
Beat[6]		-9%	60%	6%	7%

[1] The start date is 1/4/2021 and the end date is 7/1/2021.
[2] The start date is 7/1/2020 and the end date is 7/1/2021.
[3] The start date is 7/1/2016 and the end date is 7/1/2021.
[4] The start date is 1/2/2008 and the end date is 4/1/2009. My estimates.
[5] SPY is the ETF for the S&P 500 index. It is used as a yardstick.
[6] = (Avg. − SPY) / SPY. Again, it does not include fees, commissions and dividends.

Comments:
- The YTD is the only period that this portfolio does not beat SPY (the market to many). It could mean the market could

be changing the favorite from growth stocks to value stocks. However, 31% return is far above the average of the market.
- The one-year return beats the market by 60%.
- The 5-year return beats SPY only by 6%, but the return of 41% is nothing to sneeze at.
- All except Vanguard's Viper Total are ETFs for growth stocks. Hence, I expected it would not beat the market, but it still did by 7%.
- You can time the market using the techniques described in this book as often as you can. When the indicator tells you to exit, you can sell these ETFs and reenter the market when it recovers. Riskier investors can buy contra ETFs such as PSQ and SH instead of holding cash when the market is down.
- At least once in a year review the selection. Use ETFdb.com for information. If you do not have time, it is fine skipping the review. When you switch ETFs, taxes should be considered.
- Most ETFs replace some stocks periodically to ensure better appreciation potential.
- I prefer VOO due to lower fees (about .03%) fee over SPY (about .06%) for long-term investors and SPY for short-term investors due to lower spread (difference between ask price and sell price) as a larger fund.

An example

This example evaluates RING, a gold miner, using ETFdb and Finviz that are free from the web. The data is from July, 6, 2020.

Bring up ETFdb and enter RING in the search. There is basic info that are important to me: Sector (gold miners), Asset Size (Large-Cap), Issuer (iShares), Inception (Jan. 31, 2012), Expense Ratio (0.39%) and Tax Form (1099).

They fit all my requirements. The expense ratio is higher than most ETFs that simulate an index such as SPY. I try to trade ETFs using Tax Form 1099 in my taxable accounts. The large cap created about 8 years ago by a reputable company is good.

Select "Dividend and Valuation". P/E of 17.39 is fine in a rank of 11 in 27 in a similar group of ETFs. As in my books, I stated it is hard to evaluate miners. I buy this ETF primarily to fight the possibility of inflation and the potential depreciation of USD. The dividend rate of 0.52% (0.70% from Finviz) is in the low range of the scale; it is fine for me as dividend is not my concern.

There is more info from this website. For simplicity, bring up Finviz:
- The short-term trend is up (SMA-20% = 8% and SMA-50% = 7%).
- The long-term trend is up (SMA-200% = 26%).
- It is close to overbought (RSI(14) = 64%; 65% to me is overbought).
- It is -4% from 52-w High. It has performed well from the YTD, Last Year, Last Quarter, Last Month and Last Week.
- It almost doubled in price from mid-March this year.
- Avg. Vol. is fine.

From ETFdb, check the Holding. It has 39 stocks, so it is quite diversified for this industry. The two top holdings are NEM (19%) and ABX (18%), which is listed as GOLD in NYSX. I also consider buying these two stocks in addition to RING. You can estimate the other metrics that are not available by averaging these two stocks. Here is my summary:

STOCK	NEM	GOLD
Forward P/E	20	25
Debt / Share	0.31	0.24
ROE	17%	22%
Sales Q/Q	43%	30%
EPS Q/Q	389%	254%
SMA50	2%	4%
RSI(14)	59%	60%
Insider Trans	-13%	N/A

| Fidelity's Equity Summary Score | 6.1 | 6.8 |

5 Simplest market timing

Why market timing
Before 2000, market timing was a waste of time. However, after that, we have had two market plunges with the average loss of about 45%. It sounds harder to time the market than it actually is. We have a simple technique to detect market plunges and when to reenter the market. Our objective is reducing the loss to 25%.

Market timing depends on charts; the following describes how to use chart information without creating charts. Most charts will not identify the peaks and bottoms of the market as they depend on data (i.e., the stock prices). However, it would reduce further losses. It is simpler than it sounds. Just follow the procedure below.

The first part of this technique detects potential market plunges, and the second part advises you when to start reentering the market. It applies to individual stocks too. It also works to detect the trend of a sector (entering an ETF for the specific sector instead of SPY) and a specific stock.

Step-by-step procedure
When the market timer indicator (Death Cross) described next tells you to exit the market, sell SPY (an ETF simulating S&P 500). Do not forget to buy back SPY or similar ETF such as RSP, when the indicator (Golden Cross) tells you to return.

My experiences in 2000s
Basically I did the same as the above with some adaptations. I worked for a mutual fund company and they did not allow me to trade stocks effectively. However, I was allowed to trade sector funds offered by the company. Every two months, I switched to the sectors with the best performances for the last month. When most sectors were down for the last month, I rotated them to the money market fund. In March or April, 2000, I switched to traditional sectors from high-tech sectors (better to switch to market money funds). During that time, I bought stocks that had enough cash to

last more than two years judging by their burn rates. The indicators should do a better job.

How to detect market plunges without charts (similar to <u>Death Cross</u>)
1. Bring up Finviz.com.
2. Enter SPY (or any ETF that simulates the market) or RSP, equally-weighted SPY.
3. If SMA-200% is positive, it indicates that the market plunge has not been detected and you can skip the following steps.
4. The market is plunging if SMA-50% is more negative than SMA-200%. To illustrate this condition, SMA-200% is -2% and SMA-50% is -5%.
5. Another hint: B/S (buy sell ratio) is negative, specially it is more negative than last week.
6. Conservative investors should sell most stocks starting with the riskiest ones first such as the ones with negative earnings, high P/Es and/or high Debt/Equity. Obtain this info from Finviz.com by entering the symbol of the stock you own.
7. Aggressive investors should sell all stocks. Extremely aggressive investors should sell all stocks, buy contra ETFs such as PSQ, and even short stocks. I do not recommend beginners to be aggressive.

Example
As of 2/12/2022, the following are from Finviz.com.

ETF	SMA-200	SMA-50	SMA-20	Death Cross?
SPY	-0.8%	-4.2%	-1.7%	Yes (Step #4)
RSP	-0.5%	-1.9%	0.4%	Yes (Step #4)

Both ETFs indicate the market is a confirmed crash from my indications using a technique similar to Death Cross. However, they are quite close, and we should keep an eye on these numbers. In this case, SMA-20 has not been used. If it is a false alarm, the Golden Cross would indicate it and you should return to equity; it could be quite common in volatile markets. The futures indicate that on Monday (2/14/22) the market would plunge further. Another test is using SMA-350: When the current price is below SMA-300, it is a crash. SMA-20 has to be more negative than SMA-50 and it has not been used here.

Simple chart example. Bring up StockCharts.com and enter SPY. It indicates Death Cross occurred on around March 20, 2022.

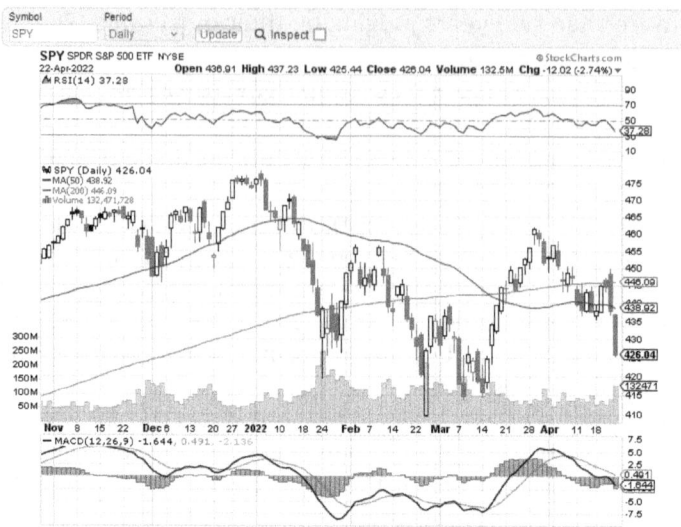

When to return to the market (similar to Golden Cross)

Use the above in a reversed sense to detect whether the market has been recovering. However, when the SMA-200% turns positive, I would start buying value stocks (low P/E but the 'E' has to be positive, and/or low Debt/Equity).

1. Bring up Finviz.com.
2. Enter SPY (or any ETF that simulates the market).
3. If SMA-200% is negative, the market is not recovering, and you can skip the following steps.
4. Sell all contra ETFs and close all shorts if you have any.
5. Market recovery is confirmed when SMA-50% is more positive than SMA-200%. To illustrate this condition, SMA-200% is 2% and SMA-50% is 5%. Commit a large percent of cash (or all cash for aggressive investors) to stocks. If you do not know what to buy, buy SPY or an ETF that simulates the market.
6. Another hint: B/S (buy sell ratio) is positive, specially it is more positive than last week.

How often should you check the market timing indicators?

Do the above once a month. When the SPY price is closer to SMA actions percentage, perform the above once a week. The charts and data for market timing described in this book are based on SMA-350 (Simple Moving Average) that is more preferable than this simple procedure, but it requires some simple charting.

Nothing is perfect

If the market timing is perfect, there would be no poor folks. The major 'defects' are:

- It does not detect the peak / bottom as it depends on past data. However, it would save you a lot during the crash.
- It is hard to determine whether it is a correction or a crash.
- From 2000 to 2010, there was only one false signal. The indicator tells you to exit and then tells you to reenter the market shortly. In most cases, you do not lose a lot. After 2010, we have more false signals.
- The market may not be rational or may be influenced due to specific conditions such as excessive printing of USD. If you do not mind charting, use SMA 350 (or 400) using SPY. Buy when the price is above SMA-350 (or SMA-400), and sell otherwise. SMA-400 reduces the number of false signals, but it is not nimble.
- I do not recommend Bitcoin but agree with most of thinking of this YouTube.
  https://www.youtube.com/watch?v=a5J8gMrEZxg

6 Rotate four ETFs

We can beat the market by rotating one ETF that represents the market such as SPY and cash via market timing. Aggressive investors can add SH or PSQ (contra ETFs) to the four to have better returns during market plunges.

During a market uptrend, rotating the following four ETFs could be more profitable than staying with SPY (or any ETF that simulates the market). Be warned that a short-term capital gain in taxable accounts is not treated as favorably as the long-term capital gain; check current tax laws.

The allocation percentages depend on your individual risk tolerance. You can use indexed mutual funds. Compare their expenses and restrictions. Some mutual funds charge you if you withdraw within a specific time period.

Select the best performer of last month (from Seeking Alpha, cnnFn, or one of many ETF/mutual fund sites). Add a contra ETF such as SH to take advantage of a falling market for more aggressive investors. Add sector ETFs to the described four ETFs such as XLY, XLP, XLE, XLF, XLU, IYW, XHB, IYM, OIL and XLU to expand your selection.

ETFs	Money Market	U.S.	International	Bond
Fidelity		Spartan Total Market	Spartan Global Market	Spartan US Bond
Vanguard		Total Stock Market	Total International Market	Total Bond Market
My choice	Fidelity	SPY	Vanguard	Fidelity
Suggest %				
During Market plunge	90%	0%	0%	10%
After plunge	10%	60%	20%	10%

Explanation

- The above are suggestions only. If your broker offers similar ETFs, consider using them.

- Check out any restrictions of the ETFs and commissions.
- 4 ETFs (one actually is a money market fund) are enough for most starters. They are diversified, low-cost and you do not need rebalancing except during a market plunge.
- The percentages are suggestions only. If you are less risk tolerant, allocate more to a money market fund, CD and/or bond ETF.
- Have at least 10% allocated to the money market fund for safety.
- When the market is risky, reduce stock equities (i.e., increase money market and bond allocations).
- The symbols for Fidelity ETFs are FSTMX, FSGDX and FBIDX.
- The symbols for Vanguard ETFs are VTSMX, VGTSX and VBMFX.
- If you are more advanced, use additional sector ETFs to rotate. Also buy long-term bond funds (such as 30-year Treasury) when the interest rate is 10% or more.

#Filler: Glad to be an investor

After watching the following YouTube video, I am glad my parents did not push me to play piano and also glad I do not have any musical gene. How can I compete with this kid?

https://www.youtube.com/watch?v=yf0B4rVoq44

Also, glad not into some life-threatening professions such as surgical doctors, soldiers, fire fighters, etc. I can make mistakes in investing from time to time without suffering from the consequences. With the uptrend market for most of the last 50 years, most investors should make good money. Thank God.

#Filler: Where common sense is not common sense

Excessive printing of money is not a long-term solution. Servicing the huge debt weakens our competitiveness. The politicians just want to buy votes today and finance their campaigns. Our next generations have to pay for these huge debts.

#Filler: Cayman Island
Most global corporations are making fun of our tax system. Moving the "headquarter" to low-tax countries such as Cayman Island with a mailbox, a bank account and/or an office that has never been used is a norm. The profitable Boeing has negative tax liability. What a shame!

8 The best strategy

The best-kept secret in investing is to buy a weighted ETF. I use SPY as an example here. This ETF is well diversified as it keeps all 500 stocks in the S&P 500 index. The ETF has a higher position (in percentage) on stocks with higher market cap. The stocks with higher market caps usually grow the market cap by having good management and good products. The bad stocks are deleted from the index periodically.

The second best-kept secret is using simple market timing as described in this book to reduce the losses in market crashes.

It is very hard to beat this strategy. You do not need any knowledge in investing, and you only spend a few minutes every month to time the market. The market is risky when the metrics show you so such as the price is close to the simple moving average in using SMA-350 method; in this case you time the market more frequently.

9 Don'ts for beginners

- Do not use leverage: options, margin and leveraged ETFs.
- Do not short stocks.
- Buy low and sell high.
- Buy value stocks. Sell profitable stocks after a year and losers before holding 12 months for favorable tax treatments in non-retirement accounts. Be a turtle investor.
- Limit momentum trades.
- Use stops to protect your portfolio.
- Do not follow 'experts' blindly (most have their own agenda).
- Do not trade penny stocks (i.e., stocks less than 200 M and/or price less than $1 to my definitions).
- Venture into momentum trading when you have knowledge and time. Avoid trading systems that are available.
- Do not day trade. Most beginners lose most of their money.
- Do not take classes / seminars that promise you big money - if it works, they will give out their secrets.
- Be selective on investing subscriptions. If they give you a handful of stocks to thousands of subscribers, most likely the actual performance will not be good. Check their past performances that use real money.
- Beginners (even some experts) miss many opportunities by only buying blue chips and/or the companies they know.

- Do not buy stocks making new lows, as there could be another bottom.
- Buy stocks on their way up, especially when the market is in an uptrend with low inflation and low interest rates.
- Do not buy products from financial planners and/or promoters but pay them for advice. Avoid annuities and some insurance products unless you have good reasons. If the promoter gets a 10% commission or a 2% front-loaded mutual funds (and some may switch funds annuity making him 2% richer every year), run as fast as you can.

Link
Common mistakes: https://www.youtube.com/watch?v=zkNueyFs8zQ

10   Summary

The following improves the odds of success but there is no guarantee.

Risky Market?
Bring up Finviz.com. Enter SPY. If both SMA-50% and SMA-200% are both negative, do not invest especially when SMA-50% is more negative than SMA-200%.

Evaluate value stocks from others' researches
Gather a list of stocks from screens and/or recommendations from magazines. Use researches that are free. Value stocks should be kept for at least 6 months. In six months or so, evaluate the bought stocks again to see whether you want to sell the stocks. Some other sites may provide free trial or one-time evaluation: IBD, GuruFocus, Zacks and Morningstar. Fidelity requires an account but there is no minimum position.

Name	Pass Grade
Fidelity's Equity Summary Score	>=8
Value Line[2]	Timeliness > Average
	Proj. 3-5 yr.% > 5%
VectorVest[1]	VST > 1 and RV > 1

[1] Should be available from your local library.
[2] Free for limited number of stocks and free trial.

Evaluate stocks
Bring up Finviz.com and enter the stock symbol.

Metric	Passing Grade
Forward P/E	Between 5 and 20 (25 for tech stocks)
P/FCF	< 15 and ratio is positive
Sales Q/Q	>10
EPS Q/Q	>15

Intangible Analysis

Bring up Finviz, Fidelity, Yahoo!Finance or Seeking Alpha (fewer articles now) and enter the stock symbol. To prevent manipulation, the stocks should have larger cap (> 200 M) and higher daily average volume (> 10,000 shares).

#Filler: The Ten Commandments of Investing.
http://www.investopedia.com/articles/basics/07/10commandments.asp

- Set goals. * Personal finances in order. * Ask questions. * Do not follow the herd. * Due diligence. * Be humble. * Be patient. * Be moderate. * No unnecessary churning. * Be safe. * Do not follow blindly.

- My additions: * Diversify. * Study market timing. * Protect your losses and profits. * Monitor your screens and your metrics. * Be emotionally detached from investments.* Learn from mistakes. * Stay away from bubbles. * Be socially responsible.

Book 2: Finding Stocks

There are approximately 4,000 stocks, or about 30,000 if you include smaller stocks and those on foreign exchanges. How can you find the winners? Screening stocks can give you a manageable list of candidates worth your further evaluation.

Finding Stocks is a practical guide to identifying profitable investment opportunities in the stock market. The book emphasizes the importance of stock screening, offering various techniques and tools to filter thousands of stocks down to a manageable list of potential winners. It explains different screening strategies, including value, growth, and momentum investing, while highlighting the significance of market cycles and economic conditions in stock selection.

The book provides an in-depth look at popular free and paid screening tools such as Finviz, Yahoo! Finance, Fidelity and AI, showing how to use them effectively. It also explores advanced screening techniques, combining fundamental and technical analysis to refine stock choices further. Additionally, the book warns about common pitfalls in investing, such as market manipulation, sector-specific risks, and the limitations of hedge funds.

With practical examples and step-by-step guidance, *Finding Stocks* equips both beginner and experienced investors with the knowledge to develop their own screening strategies, back-test their selections, and improve their decision-making process in the stock market.

Link: Five steps in investing
https://www.youtube.com/watch?v=-i-MS4nX5G4

1 Where the websites are

- **Free and simple screen sites**

    They are described in this article or type the following
    http://stocks.about.com/od/researchtools/a/071909screenlist.htm

    - Yahoo!Finance.
      Click here or type
      http://screener.finance.yahoo.com/stocks.html

    - Finviz.
      Click here or type
      http://Finviz.com/screener.ashx

      How to scan using Finviz (YouTube).
      https://www.YouTube.com/watch?v=aQ_0FTg9Cfw

      Screening using technical indicators (particularly useful for momentum stocks).
      https://www.YouTube.com/watch?v=RZRP2NeSX0s

    - Your broker.
      Fidelity's screens are more sophisticated than most.

    - More options: Google, CNBC.com and Moringstar.com.

    Here is a list.
    http://stocks.about.com/od/researchtools/a/071909screenlist.htm

- **Sophisticated screens (usually not free)**

    Most of them are more complicated and need time to learn. Both VectorVest and Stock123 provide historical databases for back testing your screens. Zacks has an earnings revision database at extra cost. GuruFocus has an easy-to-use but powerful screen function.

AAII provides screened stocks from various screens in its low-priced subscription. Both AAII and Value Line take care of some specific industries, but they provide no historical database at least for regular subscriptions. AAII provides historical performance summaries of their screens included in its subscription.

Afterthoughts

Here are the links to screens provided by MarketWatch and NASDAQ.
http://www.marketwatch.com/tools/stockre...
http://www.nasdaq.com/reference/stock-sc...

How to find quality stocks.
http://seekingalpha.com/article/2381395-how-to-identify-quality-stocks-and-is-there-really-alpha-to-be-had

Swing trading:
https://www.youtube.com/watch?v=cMmW12Smmt4

Filler
"Sell in May" could be a self-fulfilled prophecy. I prefer to sell on April 1 and come back on Oct. 15 to avoid the herd.

Filler: Happy Mother's Day Poem

The following is my translation from poet Yu's work in Chinese. I changed some words as some could not be translated effectively. I added the title "Two Cries".

-------- Two Cries -----------

I cried at two unforgettable times in my life.

The first time when I came to this world.
The second time when you left this world.

The first time I did not know but from your mouth.
The second time you did not know but from my heart.

Between these two crises, we had endless laughs.
For the last 30 years, we had joyful laughs that had been repeated, repeated...

You treasured every laugh.
I cherish every laugh for the rest of my life.

2 Finviz.com screener

You should use fundamental metrics for fundamental stocks, growth metrics for growth stocks, momentum metrics for momentum stocks, or a combination. Basically, you want to keep the fundamental stocks longer so the market would realize their values.

Finviz.com provides a screening function incorporating both fundamental and technical metrics and is one of the best free sites. Bring up Finviz.com in your browser and select screener. You have 4 tabs: Descriptive, Fundamental, Technical and All. It has the following features:

- The criteria specified can be saved but the number is limited.
- The searched stocks can be saved in a portfolio (for paper trading and performance monitoring).
- Technical indicators.
- For an extra fee, you can have a historical database. This would help you to test your strategies. The historical database is quite limited for some technical parameters only.
- Some advanced technical indicators work well, especially useful in momentum trading.
- Use technical patterns. My favorites are Head and Shoulder and Double Bottoms (Peaks).
- Combine fundamental metrics and technical metrics to narrow down your selection.
- Combine fundamental metrics and technical metrics to narrow down your selection.
- Add Insider Trans (> 5% for me), Short Squeeze (> 20%), etc. for specific purposes.
- Candlesticks is hard to master. You need to read a book dedicated to it.

http://www.investopedia.com/terms/c/candlestick.asp
https://www.youtube.com/watch?v=FsqoV1aVrUc

https://www.youtube.com/watch?v=vQHAOcKVmA0

Finviz's screener lacks the following features:

- Stocks with prices trending up in the last several weeks (such as increasing X% in the previous week).

- Using exponential moving averages that supposedly have better predictive power than simple moving averages for momentum investing.
- Selecting ranges such as selecting all three major exchanges and market cap ranges.
- P/E for an ETF. It can be obtained from other sources such as ETFdb.com.
- When the earnings (E) are negative, you may have the wrong values for P/E and the metrics using E. For example, if you want stocks with P/E less than 20, the screener returns you stocks with negative earnings.
- Combine fundamental metrics and technical metrics to narrow down your selection.
- There is no historical database that is primarily used for testing screens (the Elite version has historical databases for technical as of this writing).

All of these missing features can be worked around. The paid version provides better functions.

A screener example

The following is an example. Fine tune the selection criteria according to your personal criteria and risk tolerance.

- Bring up Finviz.com from your browser. Select Screener, the third tab. As of 3/24/2015, we have 7066 stocks.
- For illustration purposes, we would like to find stocks with double bottoms, a positive technical indicator. Select the Technical tab. Select Pattern and then Double Bottom. Now we have 257 stocks.
- Select the Fundamental tab that is next to the Technical tab. Select Forward P/E and then select "under 20". Now, we have 86 stocks.
- Select Debt/Equity less than .5. Now, we have 45 stocks. Some industries such as utilities are traditionally high in debt, so you can use 'less than 1'.
- Select EPS growth Q-to-Q over 10%. Now, we have 19 stocks.
- Select the Description tab. Select Country to USA. Now, we have 17 stocks.
- Select Price > 1. Select Avg. Volume "Over 100K". Select Float Short "Under 10%. Select Analyst Recs. "Buy or better". Now we have 9 stocks.

Now we can evaluate them one by one using Fundamental Analysis, Intangible Analysis, Qualitative Analysis and Technical Analysis. The purpose of screening is to filter the 7000 stocks to a small number (9 stocks in this case).

Skip the stocks that have the Earnings Date within 2 weeks. If you already have too many stocks in the same industry, skip that stock. You can save the screen when you have registered with Finviz.com. It is free. Check the performance of your selections after 3 months or so.

Other sources

Paper trade and check the actual performance before investing your money. Many popular screens provided by many sites worked before but may not work now. It could be too many folks using the same strategy. Hence it is important to check the current performances of the screen you are using. For yardstick, use SPY or similar ETF that simulates the market. Here are some sources beside Finviz.com.

Your broker
Most broker sites have screen functions. Some have screens to simulate what a specific guru such as what Warren Buffett would buy.

IBD (a subscription service)
From my check on the IBD 50, they're good in the last 10 years, but not that good in the last 5 years – the victim of their own success? They provide stocks from their screens. Most screens are for momentum stocks and large caps. Here are the updated days for specific lists as of this writing.

Stocks Group	Published
Sector Leaders	Daily
Stock spotlight	Daily
Top World	Daily
IBD 50	Mon. and Wed.
Weekly Review	Fri.
Big Cap 20	Tue.

You may want to check out individual stocks with Stock Checkup and then analyze them again. The following are good parameters: Composite Rating, Industry Ranking (finer and better than Sector Ranking) and Relative Price. Understand their parameters and apply accordingly - the same for most other vendors.

IBD prefers large and growing companies with institutional ownership. Some of their parameters may not make sense for small, value and/or turn around companies.

Common parameters

Different styles of investing use different parameters for screening stocks. Here is my suggested group of parameters for using Finviz.com. Vary them to your risk tolerance and market conditions. Finviz.com is not complete in all functions, but it could the best free screener that incorporates both the fundamental and the technical criteria. The first table is for Value and the next one for Growth. The last one is for finding stocks that the institutional investors are trading.

Screening value stocks

Value Screens	Common	Penny	Micro Cap	Dividend
General				
Market Cap (M)	>500 M	<50 M	50 -200 M	+Mid(>2B)
Price	>5	< 5	1-15	>5
In all 3 Exchanges	In	Not In	Most are In	In
Avg. Volume	>100K	>5K	>10K	>100K
Country	USA	USA	USA	USA
Dividend%				>3%
Float Short	<10%	<10%	<10%	<10%
Analyst Rec	Buy or +	Buy or + if avail.	Buy or +	Buy or +
Fundamental				
Forward P/E	<20	<20	<20	<25
ROE	>10	>10	>5	>15
QQ earning	>0			>0
QQ sales	>0			>0
PEG	<1	<1	<1	<1.2
Payout%				20-50%
P/S	<10	<10	<10	<10

Technical				
Price above 200 SMA	Yes	Yes	Yes	Yes
RSI(14)	< 70	< 70	< 70	< 70

There may be no analysts or very few following penny stocks and micro-cap stocks. QQ is quarter to quarter.

Screening Growth Stocks

Growth Screen	Common	Technical	Momentum
General			
Market Cap (M)	>50	> 1,000	>500
Price	>1	>10	>5
Exchanges (Major 3)	In	In	In
Avg. Volume	>50K	>200K	>100K
Fundamental			
Forward P/E	<30	<30	<30
Return of Equity	>5	>0	>0
QQ earning	>10%	>15%	>20%
QQ sales	>5%	> 5%	>10%
PEG	<1	<1	<1
Analyst recs.	Buy or +		
Technical			
Price above 200 SMA	Yes	Yes	
50 SMA	Yes	Yes	Yes
RSI	< 75	< 75	

Short-term trends are important for momentum stocks.

Explanation
The above are suggestions only. Adjust them to your personal preferences and risk tolerance.
- Finviz screener lacks ranges, such as market cap and multiple of exchanges. Most Finviz's parameters do not have a range option such as Exchanges, so you need to run the screen three times, one for each of the three major exchanges.
- Average Volume. When the price of the stock is less than $3, double the average volume requirement. In most cases, 10K is

quite acceptable to me. When the volume is small, you may have to pay more (a.k.a. spread) to trade.
- There are many fundamental metrics such as Debt/Equity and Price/Free Cash Flow that are not included here, but they should be included in your further evaluation. Each industry sector has different thresholds. For example, the P/S is very different for a supermarket rather than a high-tech company. Compare the company to the average value of the companies in the same sector. Many sites including GuruFocus.com and Fidelity.com have the average values displayed.
- For momentum stock, you can ignore most of the fundamentals and concentrate on the price trend such as SMA-20% (Simple Moving Average for the last 20 trade sessions) and SMA-50%. The higher the percent, the higher it is away from its own average. You do not want to hold momentum stocks too long (max. 3 months unless the momentum is still uptrend); personally my max. is 1 month.
- For growth stocks, ensure the PEG (P/E growth), quarter-to-quarter earnings and quarter-to-quarter sales are above the averages in its own sector and/or the market.
- Technical analysis favors large cap stocks with large volumes. I prefer stocks with positive earnings and they are fundamentally sound.
- When the SMA-20%, SMA-50% and SMA-200% are all positive, they should be in an uptrend.
- RSI(14) indicates whether the stock is oversold (>65) or under bought (<30). The range is my suggestion only.
- You may want to check out your strategies using a virtual account from your broker.
- Some websites do not have the most updated price info and that would affect many other metrics such as P/E. If they have an icon Current, check it out for the last updated date. It usually does not matter unless the stocks have big swings, such as TGT losing about 25% in one day.

A general guideline for Institutional investors

Criteria	Value
Description	
Relative Volume	Over 2 M
Country	USA usually
Institution Ownership	Over 50%

Technical	
SMA-200	>10%
Volatility	Week – Over 3%
RSI(14)	>40%
Fundamental	
Market Cap	>1B
ROE	>10%

- Again, these are my suggested metrics. I prefer USA companies and many are global companies. If you use foreign countries, ensure they are larger companies and/or in countries that have regulations similar to our SEC's.
- For value investors, select Forward P/E less than 20 (25 for high-tech companies) and their Earnings are positive.
- Check out how many analysts are following the stocks that you are interested in.

To illustrate, I find 12 stocks. I narrow them down to 3. First, I skip all stocks that already have had more than 10% rise recently. They may have risen too high already.

Select profitable stocks with forward P/E less than 25. "Debt/Equity" is less than .5 (50%). Then, ROI is higher than 25%. Stop when you have reached the optimal number of stocks (3 for me in this example). If you find too many stocks, tighten the criteria and vice versa. Save the criteria and the selected stocks in a portfolio for paper trading.

Screens for specific searches

The current free version lacks combination operations such as AND. Adjust it accordingly and you may need more than one screen to achieve the same requirements. The table includes the most important parameter(s) only.

Purpose	Criteria	Value
Long:		
Insider	Insider transactions	Very positive

Momentum	50-Day Simple Moving Avg.	Price > SMA-50
Double Bottom	Pattern	Double Bottom
Short:		
Short	20-Day Simple Moving Avg.	Price < SMA-20
Double Top	Pattern	Double Top
Information:		
Earnings Announcement	Earnings date	Next week

Links
Basic Finviz https://www.youtube.com/watch?v=cHNUMPgEYGY
https://www.youtube.com/watch?v=3la_e6D1-XA

Under YouTube, search "Finviz".
Recommended YouTube:
https://www.youtube.com/watch?v=CJoN7wLfWNo
Short-term parameters:
https://www.youtube.com/watch?v=BvMzYyynaol

Investopedia.
http://www.investopedia.com/university/features-of-Finviz-elite/other-chart-features.asp

How to scan using Finviz (YouTube).
https://www.YouTube.com/watch?v=aQ_0FTg9Cfw
Finviz's screener tutorial.
https://www.youtube.com/watch?v=glMtwB7OVf4
https://www.youtube.com/watch?v=tHtovnCY6uY
(Recommended)
Swing trading: https://www.youtube.com/watch?v=M8sNMhPJINU
Screening using technical indicators (YouTube).
https://www.YouTube.com/watch?v=RZRP2NeSX0s

Filler: Chicken feet, lobsters and trade war
Lobsters are literally flown to China for the rich. The trade war changes all these. Chicken feet, a delicacy for the Chinese, will be thrown into the ocean. I can finally enjoy a $12 plate of lobster in Boston.

Many farmers have gone bankrupt as the banks do not loan them money to buy seeds for the next year. Our storage is over-flowed. Soybeans and pork are rotting. Trump's subsidies will not help a lot for farms who have small farms and he is going to lose all the votes from these farm states.

Overview of Finviz.com

This article is written by DeepSeek (AI).

Finviz.com (short for Financial Visualizations) is a powerful and user-friendly financial visualization tool that provides investors with a comprehensive suite of tools for stock screening, market analysis, and portfolio management. It is widely used by both individual and professional investors to make informed investment decisions.

Key Features:
1. **Stock Screener**:
    - **Customizable Filters**: Finviz offers a highly customizable stock screener with over 60 filters, including fundamental metrics (P/E ratio, EPS, dividend yield), technical indicators (SMA, RSI, MACD), and descriptive criteria (sector, industry, market cap).
    - **Predefined Screens**: Users can choose from a variety of predefined screens such as "Most Active," "Top Gainers," "Top Losers," and "Unusual Volume."
    - **Visualization**: The screener results can be displayed in a table, chart, or heatmap format, making it easy to spot trends and patterns.
2. **Market Overview**:
    - **Real-Time Data**: Finviz provides real-time data on major indices, futures, and forex markets.
    - **Heatmaps**: The heatmap feature visually represents the performance of stocks and sectors, allowing users to quickly identify the best and worst performers.
    - **Charts**: Interactive charts for indices, sectors, and individual stocks are available, with various technical indicators and drawing tools.
3. **Portfolio Management**:
    - **Portfolio Tracker**: Users can create and manage multiple portfolios, track

performance, and receive alerts on price changes and news.
- **Performance Analysis**: Detailed performance metrics and charts help users analyze their portfolio's strengths and weaknesses.

4. **News and Analysis**:
   - **Latest News**: Finviz aggregates news from various sources, providing the latest updates on stocks, sectors, and the overall market.
   - **Insider Trading**: Information on insider transactions is available, helping users gauge insider sentiment.
   - **Analyst Ratings**: Analyst recommendations and price targets are provided for individual stocks.

5. **Advanced Features**:
   - **Backtesting**: While Finviz does not offer full backtesting capabilities, users can manually test strategies by saving screener results and tracking performance over time.
   - **Alerts**: Customizable alerts for price changes, volume spikes, and other criteria help users stay informed without constant monitoring.

User Experience:

- **Ease of Use**: Finviz is designed to be intuitive and user-friendly, with a clean interface and easy navigation.
- **Free and Elite Versions**: Finviz offers a free version with robust features and an Elite version ($39.50/month or $299.50/year) that includes additional features like real-time data, advanced screening options, and more frequent updates.

Benefits of Using Finviz.com:

- **Comprehensive Data**: Access to a wide range of financial data and analysis tools in one platform.
- **Visualization**: Heatmaps and charts make it easy to interpret complex data and identify trends.

- **Customization**: Highly customizable filters and screens allow users to tailor the tool to their specific needs.
- **Efficiency**: Saves time by consolidating data and tools that would otherwise require multiple sources.

Limitations:
- **Historical Data**: Finviz does not provide extensive historical data for backtesting strategies.
- **Survivorship Bias**: The platform does not account for delisted or bankrupt companies, which can affect the accuracy of performance analysis.

Conclusion:
Finviz.com is a versatile and powerful tool for investors looking to enhance their market analysis and stock screening capabilities. Its comprehensive data, customizable features, and user-friendly interface make it an invaluable resource for both novice and experienced investors. While it has some limitations, its strengths far outweigh them, making it a go-to platform for financial visualization and analysis.

3   Sectors to be cautious with

There are many reasons to be very cautious when investing in the following sectors. However, Technical Analysis (a.k.a. charting) would give you more hints than the fundamentals for stocks in these sectors.

Loan companies/banks
The financial statements do not show the quality of their loan portfolios. Banks should make easy money when you compare the CD rates to the mortgage rates. However, they could lose money in the following: 1. Default of loans / mortgages that happen frequently during recessions. 2. Banks are making risky investments that fail such as Bitcoins. 3. Investing in losing vehicles, such as the 'safe' Treasuries during rapid interest hikes (happened in 2023). 4. Poor management and/or frauds. Following this advice, you may be able to skip the banks that melted down in 2007. The peak of Citigroup was $550 and several banks including Lehman Brothers went bankrupt.

To protect ourselves, do not have one bank account with our assets over $250,000, which is protected by FDIC. Be careful on foreign banks, especially the small ones and those that are not protected by FDIC.
https://www.youtube.com/watch?v=qmpVABboOKQ

Failure of Silicon Valley Bank in 2023. If Biden did not mention about paying deposits back in full (many companies have deposits more than the insured amount), it would have shaken our financial system and the entire economic system. The failure is partly due to the rapid interest rates hikes and partly due to the loss of the loans from startup companies in a slowdown in the tech sector. Any unlawful insider trading? Be cautious on small banks; in 2008, about 1/3 of the small banks failed. I expect money from small banks would move to precious metals and larger banks.
https://www.youtube.com/watch?v=atIyLIP9sFs

Drug (generic is ok)
Understanding the complexities of the drug pipelines, its potential profits for new drugs and the expiration of its current drugs may not be worth the effort for most retail investors. In addition, a serious lawsuit and / or a serious problem with a drug could wipe out a good percentage of the stock price. When a drug shows unpromising sign(s) in any trial phase, the stock could plunge and vice versa.

Miners
It is extremely difficult to estimate how much ore (sometimes a miner owns several different types of ores and/or of different grades in the same or different mines) that the company has. It is further complicated by the complexities to extract and transport them. When the total of these costs is greater than its production price, the company will not be profitable. Understanding the market for ore futures is another discipline.

Many mining companies are in foreign countries such as Canada, Australia and countries in South America. Their financial statements of Canada and Australia are more trustworthy than those from most other emerging countries.

One potential problem of mining companies from many emerging countries is nationalization.

Mining rare earth ore is extremely risky when the profit depends on how China, a major producer of these ores, will price its ores. After China announced the export restrictions on rare earth elements, several non-Chinese companies announced to reopen their mines for rare earths but few have made any profits as of 2013. Developed countries have stricter environmental regulations. Coal suffers from the rising use of cleaner oil and gas.

Insurance companies. Insurance companies profit by:
1. The difference between the total premiums received and the total claims minus expenses in running the company.
2. How well they invest your premiums; you pay your premiums earlier than you may collect from the claims.

They can protect the profits in #1 by restricting claims by natural disasters such as earthquakes and by re-insuring. However, a bad disaster could wipe out a lot of their profits.
Even if the insurance company shows you its investment portfolio, most of us, the retail investors, do not have the time and expertise to analyze it.

Emerging countries (not a sector)
Their financial statements especially from small companies cannot be trusted and many countries use different accounting standards. Emerging countries are where the economic growth is. I trade FXI, an ETF, rather than individual Chinese companies. I have lost a lot in small Chinese companies due to fraud. To check out whether the stock is an ADR, try ADR.COM.
https://www.adr.com/

Stocks with low volumes (not a sector)
Most likely you pay a high spread to trade these stocks. They can be manipulated easier. I remember when I had a hard time trying to sell a stock of this kind. The majority of this company is owned by one person.

For simplicity, I trade stocks with the average daily trade volume over 6,000 shares (double it if the price is $2 or less). A better way could be in calculating the percent of your trade quantity / average daily trade volume to reduce the effect of penny stocks that have larger volumes due to the low prices. You need special skills to trade these stocks but it could be very profitable.

Good business and bad business
Banking is a good business. My deposit in them makes virtually zero interest, and they loan the same money making 3%. If they are more selective in loaning my money, they should make a good profit.

Restaurant is an easy business to open/run, but it is very hard to make good money. With the rising of minimal wages, it will get even tougher. That could be the reason for so many coupons today. The high-end restaurants are doing better due to the rising stock market. As of 8/2014, the newcomers Noodles & Company (NDLS) and Potbelly (PBPB) are not doing very well.

Retailing is a tough business. Looking at the top 10 retailers 15 years ago, I can only find two including Macy's that are still surviving. Most are either bankrupt or being acquired. Even Macy's was at one time in financial trouble.

Airlines are a tough business. You can tell by the average increase in fares in the last 10 years. It cannot even beat inflation. They have to charge you for everything. The next frontier charge is the restroom (especially for long-distance flights). Now I understand why they call themselves "Frontier Airline". As of 2014, it is quite profitable due to mergers and lower fuel cost.

There are several software companies that produce software such as virus detecting programs and tax preparation software. The customers faithfully buy new versions every year. That's great business.

Afterthoughts
As of 8/2013, is the emerging market oversold?
http://seekingalpha.com/article/1658252-have-emerging-markets-gotten-oversold
When an index of an emerging market is up by 10% and the currency exchange rate to USD is down by 20%, then it is not profitable.

Links
Nationalization:
http://en.wikipedia.org/wiki/Nationalization
Spread:
http://en.wikipedia.org/wiki/Bid-offer_spread
Insurance:http://seekingalpha.com/article/1239671-property-casualty-insurance-and-reinsurance-what-you-need-to-know
Bank failure: https://www.youtube.com/watch?v=FRWMsGJ2-NE

Filler: Irresponsible is my best defense
I told my date that I would not be responsible after the second drink due to the lack of an enzyme.

4 GuruFocus

There are many interesting features in Gurufocus.com. It provides the recent stock picks from gurus. Gurus have evaluated the stocks and you just follow them. Gurus' picks and insiders' purchases are one of the best picks without doing a lot of work yourself. It will not replace my production system in evaluating stocks, but it should supplement and improve my system.

They provide a very comprehensive screener and several screens to simulate what gurus would pick. If you do not have any paid subscription, this one is recommended. Take the free offer to see whether it is useful to you. I have not been paid by any one of them except those free subscriptions and /or services that are for my evaluation.

They do not have a historical database for me to test how effective my screens are. For the price they're charging, I do not complain.

They have a choice on the S&P 500 index, but not a choice of exchanges. They do not have Average Volume. It is effective to find the stocks, but you need further evaluation. Gurufocus.com provides a lot of information on a specific stock and some are quite unique such as the F-Score and the warning messages of a stock.

5 Piotroski's F-Score

Piotroski's system is an interesting strategy. I first noticed it from a screen from AAII, which is very selective. Hence, most of the time I do not find any stock using this screen. In addition, AAII recommends you to sell the purchased stocks if they fail to meet the criteria. Its F-Score is described in the following SA article:

"Here are the nine variables used to calculate the F-Score. Each variable gets scored a one (1) if the condition is met.

1. Positive (+) net income in the current year.
2. Positive (+) cash flow from operations in the current year.
3. Return on Assets [ROA] is higher in the current period compared to the previous year.
4. Cash flow from operations exceeds net income before extraordinary items.
5. Lower ratio of long-term debt to assets in the current period compared to the previous year.
6. Higher current ratio this year compared to the previous year.
7. Company did not issue new shares/equity in the preceding year.
8. Higher gross margin compared to the previous year.
9. Higher asset turnover ratio year on year.

Piotroski only selected stocks that had an F-Score higher than 6 (i.e., 7 to the maximum of 9)."

Gathering the above information is quite time-consuming. However, Gurufocus's "All-in-one-Screener" includes F=Score.

Gurufocus.com's (http://www.gurufocus.com/)

To illustrate, on 11/13/2013, I found the following 12 stocks: SGA, EXAC, ODC, FRS, ANEN, BGFV, LBMH, LDL, RUTH, LWAY, ITRN and GHIFF with the following criteria:

1. F-Score 8 or higher.
2. Market Cap between $100 M and $500 M.
3. Financial Strength between 7 and 10.

The market cap is selected as most institutional investors will not evaluate these stocks.

My modification using their concept

Most readers do not have GuruFocus. The modifications resemble the original criteria and you can incorporate them to your screener including Finviz.com. In general,

- Add negative numbers.
- Adaptive criteria as described in the book. We omit the criteria that do not work in the current market.
- Add ratios that are not available in Piotroski's era.

The first line is the original and it is followed by my changes (if any). Use Finviz.com. Most screeners use Null value for unavailable data, and some use Zero which is a mistake.

1. Positive (+) net income in the current year.
   P/E is positive and less than 25: Add 1.
   P/E is null (or zero) or negative: Minus 1.

1. Positive (+) cash flow from operations in the current year.
   P/FCP is positive: Add 1.
   P/FCP is null or negative: Minus 1.

2. Return on Assets [ROA] is higher in the current period compared to the previous year.
ROA > 10: Add 1.
ROA < 2: Minus 1.

3. Cash flow from operations exceeds net income before extraordinary items. (Not used).
4. Ratio of long-term debt to assets in the current period compared to the previous year.

    Debt/Eq < .25: Add 1.
    Debt/Eq > .75: Minus 1.
5. Current ratio this year compared to the previous year.

    Current Ratio > 1.5: Add 1.

    Current Ratio < .8: Minus 1.

6. Company did not issue new shares/equity in the preceding year. (Not used.)
7. Gross margin compared to the previous year.

    Profit Margin > 15%: Add 1.

    Profit Margin < 5%: Minus 1.

8. Prefer high asset turnover ratio year compared to the previous year.

#3, #6 and #8 are not applicable to me or hard to find equivalent ratios. They are replaced with the following criteria.

1. Short Float < 5: Add 1.
    Short Float > 15 and < 25: Minus 1.
2. Sales Q/Q > 10: Add 1.
    Sales Q/Q < 2: Minus 1.
3. EPS Q/Q > 5: Add 1.
    EPS Q/Q < 1: Minus 1.
4. SMA50 > 10%: Add 1.
    SMA50 < -10%: Minus 1.

I called it FM-Score (M for modification).

Another alternative is to use the color code (green, black and red) from Finviz.com. For example, P/FCF in green color is 'Add 1', P/FCF in red is 'Minus 1', and no score for black color.

Need to adjust to specific industries. Supermarket has high turnovers but low profit margins. Utilities have high debts.

Links
F-Score System:
http://www.investopedia.com/terms/p/piotroski-score.asp

SA article:
(http://seekingalpha.com/article/1806542-a-dividend-portfolio-built-using-the-piotroski-f-score

6   NASDAQ

It is quite similar to GuruFocus's screens in some aspects, but quite simplified. Currently it is free. Bring up Nasqaq.com from your browser. Select "Investing" and then "Guru Screeners".

The following is an illustration on 6/9/2016. Select "P/E Growth Investors" and change "Some" to "Strong". Click on "Go".

I had 5 stocks with "Strong": THO, MPX, GGAL (ADR), BRDCY (ADR) and BMA (ADR). If you prefer U.S. companies only, you only have THO and MPX and both had a desirable "Proj. P/E" under 20.

Alternatively to reduce the number of screened stocks, include stocks with "Some Strong". Sort the "Proj. P/E" in ascending order. If it is blank, most likely it is losing money or there is no estimate for this stock. Use Finviz.com or Yahoo!Finance to confirm.

PEG (P/E growth) is a growth metric and it is available for sorting. You need to evaluate each screened stock. For example, a low P/E stock may not be good if it has excessive debt, or serious pending lawsuits.

Click on the stock THO. It explains how Peter and other gurus score this stock. If you use 70% as a passing grade, 7 gurus rate it a pass and 3 gurus rated it failed.

Click on "Detailed Analysis". Peter rates 4 "Pass" and 2 "Neutral" together with the description.

Try other gurus and select the guru(s) who fit your requirements. For example, if you are a value investor, find a guru or gurus using value metrics.

7   Fidelity

Fidelity offers a strong screen function. The most unique feature is incorporating its Equity Summary Score (used to be Analyst's Opinion) and some outside researches such as Zacks and Ford.

From the main menu, select "News and Research", "Stocks" and then "Lauch stock screen" (under "Find stocks" sub-window).

The following example selects stocks with the following criteria: Security Price (2 to 250), Market Cap. (300 and above), Equity Summary Score (8 and above), Zacks (Strongest) and Ford (Strongest).

It displays the 10 stocks. Research each stock. Read the News about each stock. You may want to use Finviz.com, Yahoo!Finance and other sources to double check.

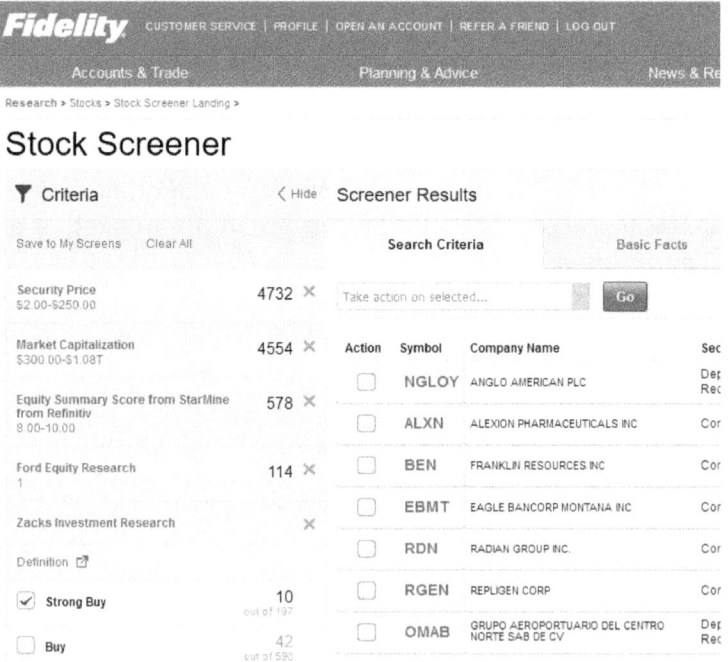

The following describes some of the features.

- Equity Summary Score. It is one of the major metrics I use in my proprietary scoring systems. They are not available to many small stocks. From my limited database in 7/2015 and for short durations, the results are:

Short Term: (7% return for the average)

Metric	Parm. 1	No. of Stocks	%	Parm. 2	No.	%	Predictability
Equity Summary Score	Buy	150	10%	Sell	279	3%	Good

Long Term: (8% return for the average)

Metric	Parm. 1	No. of Stocks	%	Parm. 2	No.	%	Predictability
Equity Summary Score	Buy	90	17%	Sell	208	4%	Good

It has its own limits, but they are very minor to me. First, it does not have a historical database for verifying the screen performance such as the return after a year. However, I do not know any site that provides this function free. To work around this, I save the results in a spread sheet and update the performance.

Secondly, it does not provide many other filter criteria that can be found in other systems such as technical indicators or insider transactions found in Finviz.com. I use other sites for further evaluation.

Most investors should find that this screening is a very good tool and very easy to use.

More info:
Under YouTube, search "Fidelity".
Recommended YouTube:
https://www.youtube.com/watch?v=fxE5577LaxE
Filler
Starbucks is being sued for too many ice cubes in the ice coffee. If he wins, he would sue MacDonald's, Burger King... and be a billionaire. Why did I not think of this? The lady won for the spilling of hot coffee. The jury did not know that eventually we had to pay for all of these and made the lawyers rich. Too many unproductive lawyers make it tough to operate a business

including small businesses. In many countries besides the U.S., the one who sues and loses has to pay for court expenses.

8   ChatGPT (and other AI models)

Besides Finviz and Fidelity as the major sources for gathering information, today we have ChatGPT and other similar AI systems. You can ask ChatGPT or Deepseek "What are the best sectors today", and ask Google "the ETF or stocks in that sector(s)". However, most likely their data bases **have not been outdated**. As of 2/10/2025, DeepSeek has not been banned.

Screening stocks. You can create a free account. I asked "best stocks for now", and it gave me 10 stocks. It gave me FB instead of the new name META and made me suspicious of the accuracy of the rest of its database. Currently, the database of ChatGPT is updated to 2021 as this writing, and hence it is not good to use it to evaluate stocks. Most are high-tech and all are large companies. It could lead to many asking the same questions and it would result in these stocks rising consequently. Watch out for the flood of selling these stocks, when they are no longer recommended.

You need to be careful how current is the database the AI model reads. Recently, DeepSeek's data was about 6 **months old,** and hence the recommendation was outdated. In Jan., 2025, both ChatGPT and DeepSeek recommended NVDA that was down by 17% on the day AI stocks crashed. We should still use it for a second opinion at best.

Analyzing stocks with MSFT as an example.
Enter "Microsoft MSFT stock". It would give you general information about the stock.
Enter "Fundamental analysis". It would give you the most fundamental data on MSFT, which are appropriate for long-term holding.
Enter "Technical analysis". It would give you the most common technical data on MSFT, which are appropriate for short-term holding.

Most sites provide duplicate data. The following lists some unique data or data that can be easily accessible from the following sites.

Use Fidelity's equity summary score and at least one report for further evaluation. Comparing its P/E to the industry's P/E is helpful." Comparing to the average 5-year P/E" and "its industry" have been moved to "More" under the tab "Statistics" .

Finviz provides most data. Insider Transaction, SMAs, Shorting % … are quite easily accessible. Yahoo!Finance provides EV/EBITDA under Statistics.

ChatGPT recommendation

You can create a free account. I asked "best stocks for now", and it gave me the following stocks. It gave me FB instead of the new name META and made me suspicious of the accuracy of the rest of its database. The current database was updated to 2021. Most of the recommended stocks are high-tech and all are large companies. It could lead to many asking the same questions and it would result in these stocks rising consequently. Use AI (ChatGPT and DeepSeek for example).)". However, most likely their data bases **have not been outdated**. As of 2/10/2025, DeepSeek has not been banned

ChatGPT's recommendation is based on 01/03/2022. My estimate on the performance.

Stock	6 Months	12 Months	18 months
AAPL	-22%	-31%	6%
AMZN	-33%	-50%	-23%
GOOGL	-22%	-39%	-17%
JPM	-30%	-16%	-9%
META	-50%	-63%	-16%
MSFT	-21%	-28%	1%
NVDA	-50%	-52%	41%
TSLA	-42%	-72%	-30%
XOM	33%	68%	69%
Avg	-26%	-32%	2%
SPY	-21%	-20%	-7%

Only XOM passed my proprietary score, and the above proves my scoring system works at least this time. Oil prices affecting XOM would be reduced in demand when electric vehicles replace combustion cars. JPM would suffer from the reduced number of IPOs in the current market conditions. The recent rise of NVDA and

MSFT is due to ChatGPT. GOOG would benefit using AI in their products.

More info from ChatGPT

Use MSFT for illustration. Type "Microsoft MSFT stock", then "Fundamental Analysis", "Technical Analysis" and lastly "Buy or sell". Even if the database is not updated, you still get some good information.

9   Performance of my screens

I monitor the performance of my top screens every 6 months or so. Here is my September, 2013 summary. The purpose is identifying the screens that have performed well recently. It is for illustration purposes only. All returns are annualized. They are sorted by Grand Avg. in descending order.

Screen	Last Monitor 2/13	Current Test Avg.	Long-term Avg.	Short-term Avg.	Grand Avg.	Avail.
EP	39%	66%			59%	75%
BB3	35%	70%			53%	25%
LPSER	-21%	72%			49%	75%
MN	19%	53%			45%	75%
CW	64%	49%	39%	20%	38%	100%
LR	30%	37%			35%	100%
TT	30%	26%	71%	8%	35%	100%
TV2	50%	76%	14%	19%	35%	100%
BFSCB	5%	38%			31%	100%
DO	29%	24%	30%		28%	100%
AR	56%	53%	23%	6%	28%	100%
BE	81%	44%	10%	13%	25%	100%
FA	16%	27%			25%	100%
BS5BV	21%	25%			24%	100%
SE		53%	20%	-3%	23%	100%
CAO	-3%	17%	37%	12%	21%	100%
...	...	...	---	...	...	
Avg.	34%	19%	23%	5%	19%	

Screen.
They are the abbreviations. To illustrate, CAO is the screen looking for candidates for acquisition with low market caps. I have about 25 production screens. They have been selected among over 100 screens.

Last Monitor 2/2013.
Copied from the "Current Test Avg." from my last monitor in 2/2013.

Current Test Avg.

It is the average of the four tests on recent months. The four test dates are: 03/11/13 to 7/9/13, 4/9/13 to 8/7/13, 5/9/13 to 8/17/13 and 6/8/13 to 9/6/13. They are about 4 months apart. It is the most important average to reflect what worked recently.

Long-term Avg.
It is the long-term performance (about 12 months) of the actual, screened stocks. These are stocks that have been actually screened and some may have been purchased.

Short-term Avg.
It is the short-term performance (about 6 months) of the actual, screened stocks.

Grand Avg.
It is a weighted average of the above 4 return categories (Last Monitor, Current Test Avg., Long-Term Avg. and Short-Term Avg.) and they're sorted in descending order.

Run the top screens first as they have given me better returns in the past. It does not guarantee that they will perform as well as before, but they have a better chance to perform well than the screens scored below the average.

Availability.
To illustrate, if the screen found stocks in 1 out of the 4 tests, it is 25% available. These screens may not have enough data for prediction on the future results and there is a higher chance that I will not find any stocks using these screens.

Observations
The following are the personal findings on my own screens. You can do something similar to separate your top screens from the rest of your screens. Test and monitor the performances of your own screens.

- Usually, the top half of the screens from the last monitor show up in this monitor though their ranks may vary.

- CAO in the last monitor should be better than it indicates. At least two companies had been acquired and they had very good returns. These two companies did not show up in the test as they're taken out from the historical database; it is termed as survivorship bias.

- CW is quite consistent to the last monitor.

- EP and BB3 have not found any stocks in actual usage. MN proves to be a good screen in these two performance monitors. I missed the opportunities to make good money from this screen – my mistake.

- LPSER is a risky screen demonstrated here and from the previous monitors. I prefer not to take unnecessary risk. Include a column of maximum drawdown as it is a good indicator to avoid risky screens.

- LR was below the average and that's why it had not been used. It is above the average in this monitor, so it will be used to some small extent.

- TT is above the average in these two monitors. The returns of screened stocks during this monitor are better in both long term and short term and hence it will be used.

- The original table (not shown here) has comparisons to SPY (an ETF simulating the market). Beating the market is my yardstick. If most of your screens beat the market, most likely they will beat the market again. However, there are exceptions such as when the market is plunging. In this case, value stocks are better than growth stocks, and cash is the king.

  The market during my last monitor is better than this period. If the return of SPY is negative in the last three months, there is a good chance that the market is trending down.

- There are some screens that just do not perform for a long while. They will not even be monitored next time. However, when the phase of the market cycle changes, the performance of these screens may respond differently.

- The test results are not always consistent. It could be due to my limited data, or the market does not behave normally.

10 A scoring system

This scoring system helps you to select whether you should buy a stock or not. In this system, when a stock scores higher than 2, it is a buy. As a group, the highly-scored stocks usually perform better than the lowly-scored stocks in a year. The basic concepts are described here.

An Example

For illustration purposes, we use two metrics: Forward P/E and ROI.

First, we convert Forward P/E into Forward E/P by flipping the two values. Assuming Forward E/P should have a higher weight than ROI, multiply E/P by 5. The average ROI is 10% (simplified for illustration), so minus it by .1.

   Score = Forward E/P * 5 + (ROI -.1)

For example, a stock has a P/E of 10 (E/P = 1/10= .1) and ROI is expressed as 25%.

   Score = .1 * 5 + (.25 - .1) = .5 + .15= .65

Some parameters by some sites are expressed in grade such as A, B, C and D. For simplicity, if it is A, then the value is 2 otherwise it is zero.

   Score = if (Grade = "A", 2, 0) + ...

Test your system on paper with at least 3 months of data. Check whether your scoring system works. It works when the higher the score corresponds to the better the return. Adjust the weight on each metric and see whether your scoring system improves its predictability.

Again, it is simplified for educational and illustration purposes. Try even more different metrics and check whether the metrics still work in the current market. The next metrics to include could be Equity Summary Score from Fidelity, Debt/Equity and Quarter-to-Quarter Earnings / Sales.

Monitor your scoring system

I am sure that many have tried to use most of the metrics and they still cannot find the Holy Grail. I believe the predictability power of each metric is influenced by the current market conditions. For example, the fundamental metrics such as P/E predict better than the growth metrics such as PEG during the market bottom. You should test the performance of each metric every 6 months or so.

You may have two scores: one for short term and one for long term. The stocks you want to keep in the short term may not be the same kind of stocks you want to keep in the longer term. Short term is 3 months (one month for me) and the long term is 12 months for me. My definitions could be different than yours. Value metrics are more important for the long term while growth metrics are more important for the short term.

However, 12 months is too long a period of time and during this period the market may change, so it is better to change it from 12 to 6. To illustrate, energy stocks were great in 2007, but they plunged in 2008. If your scoring system for long-term holding was constructed based on 12 months' data in 2007, the system would have been misleading in 2008 for energy stocks in this example.

I find the short-term scores have a better prediction power than the long-term scores. However, I keep profitable stocks more than 12 months to qualify for the better tax treatments in taxable accounts, and sell the losers less than 12 months. Evaluate the purchased stocks every 6 months to decide whether you want to keep them for another 6 months. Use stops and trailing stops (for winners) to protect your portfolio.

Besides monitoring the metrics in your scoring system, monitor the scores.

The market is not always rational

Sometimes the scoring system fails: When the poorly-scored stocks perform better than the highly-scored stocks. The market is not always rational. Most scoring systems depend on fundamental metrics. When the market switches its favor from value to growth, adjust the score system accordingly. I have found that more than one time that the stocks scored in the top 5% did not perform, so be careful or skip the top 5% (sometimes 10%). The events such as a pending lawsuit or an expiring drug do not show up in metrics, and that is why we need to do other analysis such as Intangible Analysis.

Some metrics almost always work such as the positive predictions of excessive insider's purchases. The insiders know the company typically better than others. When they buy their own company's stock at market prices, they must know it has good appreciation potential. They have many reasons to sell their company's stocks. However, when they sell a large percent of their holdings, be cautious.

When the stock loses more than 30% in a month and you cannot find valid reasons, it may be a good indicator for potential appreciation ahead. Some suggestions are:

- Do not modify your scoring system during market plunges.
- The best strategy is to use the screens (same as searches) that have worked well for the last 90 days.
- Find out why your fundamental metrics that used to work do not work now. You may want to add more weight on growth metrics, and vice versa on value metrics.

An example of monitoring the metrics

This is what I found in monitoring the performances of the metrics as of 3/2013. It is based on a limited database of about 300 stocks with holding periods varying from 1 to 15 months. It has an average of 8% (16% for shorter term). The following is for educational purposes only.

1. The foreign stocks are not doing well: South America (average return is -21% for 7 stocks), Israel (-18% for 2), China (-10% for 7). Europe (0% for 17) and Canada (5% for 16, and most are in natural resources). If I ignore the foreign companies, the return of the portfolio would increase substantially.

2. The following metrics work fine for the long term only: Forward (same as Expected) Earnings Yield (E/P) and Fidelity's Equity Summary Score.

3. P/B. The stocks with P/B less than 1 perform better than the stocks with P/B greater than 2 (10% vs. 4%).

4. There are no definitive conclusions on Cash / Market Cap, PEG and Return of Equity (a surprise to me) in this monitor.

5. The stocks that were cheaper by 50% to their average 5-year P/E (available from Fidelity) have performed better than those stocks that were cheaper by less than 2%.

6. The ratio of Short / Market Cap between 25% and 30% has better performance than other percentages. It is a contradictory ratio and it could be a short squeeze (a condition that the stock is running out of shares to sell short).

7. There are many composite scores from different vendors that I subscribe to and they are not disclosed here.

8. Based on the above, I will modify my scoring system. I will still have two scores, one for short term and one for longer term.

Short-term scoring system

The scoring system should work better in the shorter term. For testing this system, I used the above database, but deleted stocks that have been over 8 months old. It is still a small database of about 190 stocks.

The result is different from the above as the time frame has been reduced. Here is the summary.

1. The predictability of screens (same as searches) performs about the same as the last monitor. A few screens are better than others. I will not use the under-performing screens with real money.

2. The stock grades from several vendors are not a good indicator this time.

3. Expected (same as Forward) Earnings Yield (E/P) has been a good indicator.

4. Cash Flow is a good indicator (different from the last monitor).

5. Fidelity's Equity Summary Score is a good indicator. Finviz has a similar score, but I prefer to use Fidelity's. Fidelity places higher weight on opinions from analysts that have a better prediction on this stock than others. It eliminates some of the conflict of interest between the analysts and the investing banks s/he works for.

6. The Short Percentage between 25 and 30 is a good contrary indicator (could be a good chance for a short squeeze).

    Its value of less than 10 % is a good indicator. The rest of the range is not conclusive.

7. Cash / Market Cap, Insider Purchase, P/B, ROE and Dividend stocks (>3%) are not conclusive in this monitor.

8. P/S with values less than 0.8 are a good indicator.

9. For some reason I do not know why and how to explain: the top 10% of the top-scored stocks did not perform better than the other stocks that pass.

    It happens in both my two scoring systems. Be suspicious of them and it has happened for more than once. However, the stocks that scored in the bottom 10% are consistently poor performers and that's a good indicator.

There are many other parameters that may be of interest to you. Include them in the performance monitor.

11 Hedge fund 101

Do not believe you can always make money by investing in hedge funds. Most likely, you can fare better by using a diversified ETF as many found out.

LTCM (a hedge fund named Long Term Capital Management), with smart folks, ran their hedge funds into the ground. Many hedge funds are closed due to fraud, and/or poor performance.

The primary purpose is supposed to 'hedge' your investments from market plunges / dips. Since 2008, the government has printed so much money, and it makes the market 'recover'. It also makes the hedges (shorts, derivatives, etc.) unnecessary. In reality, most hedge funds today do not hedge. Many hedge funds lost a lot of money due to shorting GameStop and AMC in 2021 (gaining some back in the last month of 2021).

Hedge funds get tons of press coverage as a Holy Grail type of investing. The media need the advertising from this $2.5 trillion industry. It is similar to mutual funds, but they take more risk for supposedly better returns. Most require higher minimum investments (many start at 1 million) and more restrictions such as requiring longer holding periods.

It could be the worst deal to most of their customers: 2% average up front (for expenses) and 20% average on your profit. It is more acceptable to me if the 20% is on profit over the S&P 500 return. Why should I pay you 20% on my 10% profit when the market rises by 15%? In this case, my fund loses 5% relative to the market.

Well, if they consistently make a lot of money for you, it may not be too much to object to. However, most risk your money by betting big recklessly. When they win, they get 20% of your profit and they use you for advertising to lure in other suckers. When they lose *your* money, they do not lose a penny. It encourages them to take big risks. I do not know any hedge fund (HF) manager who pays you back your losses. Many funds have watermarks. It means that they have to make back the previous loss before they get the 20% from the current profit. When a hedge fund loses money, most of the support analysts would leave as they expect less bonuses. The fund manager may close the fund and start another one or find another job.

You would have better return by investing in a no-load index fund, or a diversified ETF than an average hedge fund. To calculate the average hedge fund performance, you need to include the many hedge funds that are out of business. To illustrate my point, check out the performance of SPY in the last five years and that of the average hedge fund including the closed ones.

After a hedge fund has failed, most fund managers just open another hedge fund (if they do not go to jail first due to fraud) and give you all the excuses for losing your hard-earned money. Some lose their reputation, but you may not check out their past performances.

In 2011 for example, the hedge fund industry did not beat the S&P 500 index fund after their fees.

Some hedge fund managers learn modern portfolio theories from Ivy League universities and apply them in the hedge funds. Often their theories are based on wrong testing procedures, or they cannot be sustained in real life.

Many invest in new companies and small companies where they would have big profit swings. They need to learn the business of the company in which they plan to buy the stocks, interview the owners, read between the lines, and double check whether the owners are telling the truth by talking to their competitors, vendors and customers. It explains the high cost for their research. We just need to look at the transactions of the insiders. There is no need to travel to visit the company unless you want to.

Some use their specialties in certain sectors and that's fine. If they use derivatives, be careful and that's what resulted in our 2007 financial crisis. Derivatives could reduce the risk of the portfolio if they are properly used. If you still want to invest in them, ask for their methods and their historical performances. Very few hedge funds are good. When you find a good one, most likely it has been closed to new investors or its fees are outrageous.

The owner of a famous baseball franchise lost big money from a hedge fund that concentrated in the oil sector. Almost every ETF in this sector made good money that year, but he still stayed with the hedge fund and had similar miserable returns the following year. I did not blame him for his first mistake, but on his sticking with the same hedge fund after a losing year. It could be that the hedge fund gave him a hard time when he wanted to take his money out, or he could be busy with his baseball franchise.

One hedge fund has a performance of 25% every year over a long period of time. The SEC should take notes and then investigate whether they were using insiders' information. It turned out it did. There are very few hedge funds with consistent performance beating the market after their hefty fees. If you find one, stay with them forever. One hedge fund was rated as the top fund and the next year it was out of business due to poor performance. Hedge fund managers chase after short-term returns as the outflow will be serious if they do not perform well. When they were successful recently, they had a hard time performing due to an excessive inflow of money.

In 1980, this industry started with really capable fund managers and made good money for their clients. After that, every analyst wanted to open a hedge fund and most did not even beat the market after their fees. Alternatively, just buy the ETF SPY (or similar ETF for the market) and relax, instead of waiting for the hedge fund to wipe out your savings.   This   industry   is   not   properly   regulated.

Do not believe in any articles / ads praising how great the hedge funds are without knowing their credibility and their hidden agendas. The hedge fund indexes usually ignore the survivor bias of the bankrupted hedge funds and the early exits of many hedge funds.

Since the hedge funds very seldom keep the stocks for more than a year, their capital gains would be short-term and hence would be taxed at a higher rate than the long-term capital gains. In addition, many funds have a 1–3-year lock-up period and only allow withdrawals on the first day of each fiscal quarter.

How hedge funds make money

- They can short stocks. Market timing and sector timing are usually not allowed in mutual funds. Hence, they can make money in a neutral market. A retail investor can do the same.

- Merger / acquisition. Buy the stock of the company being acquired, and short sell the acquiring company. Reverse the trades when the acquisition fails. A retail investor cannot do so efficiently unless you understand the acquisition.
- Change in the index such as S&P 500. It forces some ETFs and mutual funds to trade according to the change. Some bankrupting companies, and companies not meeting the requirements (market cap, profitability...) will be removed. It is easier to track these companies than the ones that will be added. Hard for the retail investor.
- Window dressing close to the end of the month, quarter (month 3, 6, 9 and 12). If the stock price of your stock is up by 5% or more for no reason, sell it. It usually returns to the previous price shortly. The hedge fund manager usually buys more on the winners and sells the losers.
- Breakouts. It used to work fine, but not anymore. Probably it is due to more retail investors (many quit their jobs and dedicate their time in trading). The hedge fund managers could jack up the price of a specific stock to make a breakout. Then, they would unload the stock to take profits. Most of the time, the retail investors lose.
- Program trading. With the fast computers to scan a lot of data and trading automatically could make them good profits. The results are not great, but program trading with AI will be better than today for sure. Not for retailers.

Links

LTCM:
https://en.wikipedia.org/wiki/LongTerm_Capital_Management
Hedge Fund: http://en.wikipedia.org/wiki/Hedge_fund
Hedge Fund: https://www.youtube.com/watch?v=Rk7sMcmKQ-w

Filler: Toaster and the economy

You can find many toasters made in the USA in museums. Is it OK to move the toaster factories from China to Vietnam?

The logic:
All toasters are made in China.
Chinese toasters are crappy.
Conclusion: All toasters are crappy.
Question: Do you find the iPhone crappy (as it is assembled in China)?

Question: If we charge heavy tariffs on Chinese goods and the Chinese do the same on our exports such as Boeing planes (the disadvantage is to us if they do not have the same tariff on Airbuses). What is it called? Trade war.

Book 3: Evaluating Stocks

Evaluating Stocks is a detailed guide designed to help investors analyze and assess stocks effectively.

The book explores key **fundamental and technical analysis techniques**, providing insights into metrics such as price-to-earnings (P/E) ratios, earnings growth, debt levels, and market trends.

It covers **various investment strategies**, including value investing, growth investing, and momentum trading, helping readers identify which approach suits their risk tolerance and financial goals. The book also discusses industry and sector analysis, emphasizing the importance of comparing stocks within their respective markets to make informed decisions.

A major highlight is the discussion on **red flags to avoid**, such as overvalued stocks, unsustainable growth rates, and misleading financial reports. Additionally, it provides practical tools and resources, including stock screeners and valuation models, to streamline the evaluation process.

With **real-world examples and step-by-step methods**, *Evaluating Stocks* is an essential resource for both beginner and experienced investors looking to refine their stock-picking skills and improve portfolio performance

Why you need further stock analysis after screening

First, you may have too many screened stocks. Second, it is for better performance. I listed the rejected stocks (12) in my recent book "Best stocks for 2024". From 12/20/23 (the publish date) to 3/29/2024 (today). The average return of the rejected stocks is about 2%, while the RSP (an ETF for unweighted S&P 500 stocks) has a return of about 10%. The average return of the recommended 8 stocks is about 14%. There are many other examples.

How to start

First, we filter stocks from about 7,000 selected stocks available from Finviz.com for example; the number is variable from different websites and/or services. To start with, skip stocks that are not in the three major exchanges, market caps less than 50 M, or daily average volumes less than 10,000 shares.

Check out the "Simplest Way to Evaluate Stocks" in the Common Tools section to evaluate stocks for beginners and couch potatoes. Furthermore, refer to Scoring Stocks to evaluate stocks via a scoring system.

1 My Performances

They are the recommended stocks in the primary lists (for long-term stocks) of my last five books in this "Best Stocks" series:

Book	Stocks	Return	Ann.	Beat RSP by
Best stocks to buy for 2022	10	4%	4%	153%
Best Stocks to buy as of July, 2021	8	5%	13%	487%
Best Stocks for 2021 2nd Edition	10	42%	52%	220%
Best Stocks for 2021	4	29%	44%	118%
Best Stocks to Buy from Aug, 2020	14	45%	45%	3%
Avg.	9	25%	32%	196%

The details can be found in the following link.
http://tonyp4idea.blogspot.com/2022/12/best-stocks-series.html

---

Filler: Incredible coincidence

My best man met the maid of honor in my wedding and they got married later. My best man was my elementary classmate in Hong Kong. The amazing coincidence is that I met him unexpectedly in a Greyhound bus station in Albany at 3 am when I was coming to Mass. for grad school from Cal., and he was changing buses on his way to Toronto. The chance could be higher than hitting the lottery. I prefer to hit the lottery. LOL.

On our flight back from Hong Kong, the one who introduced my future wife to me was two seats away from us on the same row. I cannot believe there is no God arranging our lives.

#Filler: Nobel Prize

Deng did not get a Nobel prize for saving millions from starving to death while Obama got one for doing nothing. It explained the serious prejudice and the dumb discrimination of the committee members.

2   Amazing returns

To achieve a consistent 10% return above S&P 500 over many years is every fund manager's dream. To double one's investment above the S&P 500 return is amazing while tripling it is unheard of. I beat the S&P 500 by 700% and I can detail the history of my transactions.

Many analysts show their average yearly returns and/or their returns of their top 10 stocks this time of year. The market has closed early today on Christmas Eve, so I have the time to check my recent performance. As a trader with many trades, it would be far too complicated for me to do the same for the entire year. I selected all the stocks I purchased in the last 90 days. Most of them are deeply-valued stocks. Let's check how I performed so far on these stocks.

Whenever you have achieved a high return such as this one, take the profit as it may have reached its peaks. To me, most profits are made in swing trades with an average holding period of just 90 days.

Stocks bought and their returns as of 12/25/12

Stocks	Date Bought	Return	SPY Return
BANR	12/07/12	3%	-.13%
KTCC	12/06/12	0%	.7%
QCOR	12/07/12	15%	-.1%
KTCC	12/06/12	-1%	.7%
ACTV	12/05/12	-5%	.7%
IAG	12/05/12	-1%	.7%
ADES	12/04/12	6%	.6%
NC	12/03/12	15%	-.3%
VELT	12/03/12	64%	-.3%
ANR	11/28/12	33%	4.8%
AAPL	11/16/12	1%	4.8%
C	11/14/12	13%	3.0%
DECK	11/13/12	16%	2.7%
MSFT	11/13/12	0%	2.7%
ALU	11/13/12	38%	2.7%
DLTR	11/09/12	7%	3.4%
CAT	11/08/12	4%	1.9%
MSFT	11/07/12	-8%	.5%
BSX	10/24/12	14%	.3%
BSX	10/19/12	7%	.3%
20			
AVG:		11%	1.35%

Beat SPY (in %) = (11%-1.35%)/1.35% = 716% or 7 times

Average Return = averaging each return of 20 stocks = 11%
Average Annualized Return = 148% or 122% (= 11% *365 / avg. holding period)
Average Return = Profit / Capitalization   = 10%[1]

How the returns are calculated
Using BANR to illustrate how the return and the SPY return are calculated.

BANR	12/07/12	3%	-.13%

BANR was bought on 12/07/12 (17 days from 12/24/12) at 27.93 and it was at 30.43 on 12/24/12.
Rate of Return = (30.43 – 27.93) / 27.93 = 3%

SPY was at 142.53 on 12/07/12 and at 142.35 on 12/24/12.
  Rate of Return = (142.35-142.53) / 142.53 = -.13%

Commissions and dividends are not included for simplicity. Commissions are negligible and dividends could add about another 2% for the annual returns.

Interpreting the performance results
The quantity of each stock bought is not important as I am comparing the return of the stock. However, a few stocks have been listed twice as I bought two times usually on separate dates. If I chose them as one purchase instead of two, my return would appear even better. The purchases are real, so the amount of each stock is not identical to each other.

I'm not too excited yet. This phenomenal return could be just this one time only. 90 days is a short period. Consistency could be achieved with an improved stock picking technique, plain luck or a combination. By any measure, it is an extremely decent return. However, I do not expect to beat S&P 500 by 7 times again.

My best return is from 2009 in my largest taxable account. It was over 80% beating the SPY by about 3 times. 2003 was another good year for profit. These two years are defined by me as the Early Recovery stage in a market cycle and the market provides the best profit opportunity.

The four losers are MSFT (-8%), ACTV (-5%), KTCC (-1%) and IAG (-1%). The best winners are: VELT (64%), ALU (38%), ANR (33%) and QCOR (19%). The following are in a 14% to 16% range: DECK, NC and BSX (2 purchases). Click here for the entire list.

Cheating the results

I could 'cheat' for better results by doing the following, but I did not:

1. Exclude stocks only purchased in the last 20 days (instead of 15).

2. If my purchases of CSCO were included, the result would be even better. CSCO has been bought three times on 7/24/12 and it has gained 31% as of 12/25/12. I still have CSCO, but it is not included as it just hit the 90-days requirement.

3. I could include those buy orders that had not been executed due to their fast appreciation.

Hence, there are many ways to cheat, so you should read others' results carefully.

What stocks were included
There were 20 purchases. I bought some stocks twice and that counted as two purchases. None of the stocks have been sold as of 12/25/12. I have excluded the stocks that I am testing a strategy by trading them every month and most are in a separate account.

How the stocks were picked
The majority of the stocks were screened by my selected screens that had been proven profitable in the last 3 to 6 months, or are historically profitable at this stage of the market cycle. I also analyzed most of the screened stocks and assigned a score (15 and higher is a buy) based on the metrics that had a reliable prediction recently. I do not stick with the scoring system 100% of the time, but most of the stocks that I purchased twice have high scores.

The poor performers were scored as: MSFT with a score of 13, ACTV 16, KTCC 27 and IAG 23. The scoring system is OK. MSFT should not be bought judging from its low score. However, I believe MSFT has long-term appreciation potential. The other three are the latest purchases in this portfolio and they may perform better in a longer period of time.

The winners were scored as: VELT 34, ALU was not scored, ANR was not scored and QCOR 30. The scoring system is great for this group. ALU and ANR were selected from two Seeking Alpha articles and their selections were not based on these scores. I read several Wall Street Journal articles on ALU and CSCO to convince myself to buy both of them.

The average winners were scored as follows: DECK 9, NC 26 and BSX was not scored. DECK was selected based on an article from Seeking Alpha and it seemed DECK was experiencing the same short squeeze as CROX once did. BSX was selected from a Sunday paper article.

Observations
1. I notice that most big winners (ALU is $1) have a stock price less than $10. The myth of holding quality stocks with prices higher than $15 is not true here as most of my big winners were below $10 including ALU.
2. I did not double my normal purchases on VELT and ALU, which both turned out to be my best performers. VELT scored high in my analysis. ALU was very convincing but it seemed to be risky. 'Nothing risk and nothing gained' applies here. I did triple my purchase on CSCO, which is a large company with good fundamentals that were not yet 'discovered' by the market.

   Both AAPL and DECK gained more than 25% and then lost most of their gains during my short holding period. I should have sold AAPL as many of my fellow investors sold the winners expecting higher capital gains taxes next year. The myth of 'buy and hold' does not work here.
3. During this period, I had several buy orders that were not executed due to their rising stock prices. Market orders could be the solution. It is another example of pennies smart and a pound foolish.
4. It will be interesting to check the results again in 6 and 12 months. Except ALU, all are in my taxable accounts and I usually

keep them for a year to qualify for the lower tax rates due to capital gains.
5. I have not described any specific method, but these concepts help you to build better strategies to customize to your individual situations and/or market conditions. Invest the money you can afford to lose. Past performance does not guarantee future results.

6. Reading articles such as Seeking Alpha can be beneficial providing they are not 'bump-and-switch' scheme. However, you should do your own analysis. It is your money after all.
7. The market has been up by .8% in the last 90 days and this portfolio increased by 11%. If my portfolio amplifies the market, I wonder whether it will be down by the same rate in a down market.
8. This portfolio is quite diversified even that I have not planned that way except weighing more with high tech companies. There are no big winners and no big losers that could change the average returns.
9. I tried not to include emerging countries such as China as I do not trust their balance sheets.
10. I have never achieved such an amazing return. I'm emotionally detached to big wins and big losses. It could be plain luck. Even the best strategy will have its "black swan" moment eventually.

11. To achieve over 100% annualized return is not sustainable by checking the top performers of the S&P 500 index and their returns. However, it is possible but not likely if you churn your portfolio more than once and you time the market correctly.

12. Time to take profits as most stocks here have achieved my objectives. Use the cash to buy stocks with a similar appreciation potential. You will never go broke taking profits.

Conclusion

My three steps of making a stock purchase are: 1. Market timing, 2. Screening stocks, 3. Stock Analysis and 4. When and what to sell. They have all been discussed throughout the book. Market timing and strategy (#2 and #3) does not always work, but it will go better with using them.

I am the living proof *against* the Efficiency Theory and the claims that stock picking does not work. It may not work from time to time, but in the long run it works.

Footnote

[1] Profit / Capitalization should be a little less than 20%. The original 10% is correct when you invest all the 20 stocks at the start of the beginning of the investment period. I bought these stocks on different dates. If I assume the average time of all the stock purchases is at a mid-point, then my average capitalization is only half and hence giving a 20% return.

It is slightly less than 20% as I did not include the stocks that I bought in the last 15 days. Use the number for a comparison and that's why we have to be concerned with the performance from most investment subscriptions.

Link: Intrinsic value: https://www.youtube.com/watch?v=nX2DcXOrtuo

A scoring system

This scoring system helps you to select whether you should buy a stock or not. In this system, when a stock scores higher than 2, it is a buy. As a group, the highly-scored stocks usually perform better than the lowly-scored stocks in a year. The basic concepts are described here.

An Example

For illustration purposes, we use two metrics: Forward P/E and ROI.

First, we convert Forward P/E into Forward E/P by flipping the two values. Assuming Forward E/P should have a higher weight than ROI, multiply E/P by 5. The average ROI is 10% (simplified for illustration), so minus it by .1.

Score = Forward E/P * 5 + (ROI -.1)

For example, a stock has a P/E of 10 (E/P = 1/10= .1) and ROI is expressed as 25%.

Score = .1 * 5 + (.25 - .1) = .5 + .15= .65

Some parameters by some sites are expressed in grade such as A, B, C and D. For simplicity, if it is A, then the value is 2 otherwise it is zero.

Score = if (Grade = "A", 2, 0) + ...

Test your system on paper with at least 3 months of data. Check whether your scoring system works. It works when the higher the score corresponds to the better the return. Adjust the weight on each metric and see whether your scoring system improves its predictability.

Again, it is simplified for educational and illustration purposes. Try even more different metrics and check whether the metrics still work in the current market. The next metrics to include could be Equity Summary Score from Fidelity, Debt/Equity and Quarter-to-Quarter Earnings / Sales.

Monitor your scoring system

I am sure that many have tried to use most of the metrics and they still cannot find the Holy Grail. I believe the predictability power of each metric is influenced by the current market conditions. For example, the fundamental metrics such as P/E predict better than the growth metrics such as PEG during the market bottom. You should test the performance of each metric every 6 months or so.

You may have two scores: one for short term and one for long term. The stocks you want to keep in the short term may not be the same kind of stocks you want to keep in the longer term. Short term is 3 months (one month for me) and the long term is 12 months for me. My definitions could be different than yours. Value metrics are more important for the long term while growth metrics are more important for the short term.

However, 12 months is too long a period of time and during this period the market may change, so it is better to change it from 12 to 6. To illustrate, energy stocks were great in 2007, but they plunged in 2008. If your scoring system for long-term holding was constructed based on 12 months' data in 2007, the system would have been misleading in 2008 for energy stocks in this example.

I find the short-term scores have a better prediction power than the long-term scores. However, I keep profitable stocks more than 12 months to qualify for the better tax treatments in taxable accounts, and sell the losers less than 12 months. Evaluate the purchased stocks every 6 months to decide whether you want to keep them for another 6 months. Use stops and trailing stops (for winners) to protect your portfolio.

Besides monitoring the metrics in your scoring system, monitor the scores.

The market is not always rational

Sometimes the scoring system fails: When the poorly-scored stocks perform better than the highly-scored stocks. The market is not always rational. Most scoring systems depend on fundamental metrics. When the market switches its favor from value to growth, adjust the score system accordingly. I have found that more than one time that the stocks scored in the top 5% did not perform, so be careful or skip the top 5% (sometimes 10%). The events such as a pending lawsuit or an expiring drug do not show up in metrics, and that is why we need to do other analysis such as Intangible Analysis.

Some metrics almost always work such as the positive predictions of excessive insider's purchases. The insiders know the company typically better than others. When they buy their own company's stock at market prices, they must know it has good appreciation potential. They have many reasons to sell their company's stocks. However, when they sell a large percent of their holdings, be cautious.

When the stock loses more than 30% in a month and you cannot find valid reasons, it may be a good indicator for potential appreciation ahead. Some suggestions are:

- Do not modify your scoring system during market plunges.
- The best strategy is to use the screens (same as searches) that have worked well for the last 90 days.
- Find out why your fundamental metrics that used to work do not work now. You may want to add more weight on growth metrics, and vice versa on value metrics.

An example of monitoring the metrics

This is what I found in monitoring the performances of the metrics as of 3/2013. It is based on a limited database of about 300 stocks with holding periods varying from 1 to 15 months. It has an average of 8% (16% for shorter term). The following is for educational purposes only.

- The foreign stocks are not doing well: South America (average return is -21% for 7 stocks), Israel (-18% for 2), China (-10% for 7). Europe (0% for 17) and Canada (5% for 16, and most are in natural resources). If I ignore the foreign companies, the return of the portfolio would be increased substantially.
- The following metrics work fine for the long term only: Forward (same as Expected) Earnings Yield (E/P) and Fidelity's Equity Summary Score.
- P/B. The stocks with P/B less than 1 perform better than the stocks with P/B greater than 2 (10% vs. 4%).
- There are no definitive conclusions on Cash / Market Cap, PEG and Return of Equity (a surprise to me) in this monitor.
- The stocks that were cheaper by 50% to their average 5-year P/E (available from Fidelity) have performed better than those stocks that were cheaper by less than 2%.
- The ratio of Short / Market Cap between 25% and 30% has better performance than other percentages. It is a contradictory ratio and it could be a short squeeze (a condition that the stock is running out of shares to sell short).
- There are many composite scores from different vendors that I subscribe to and they are not disclosed here.
- Based on the above, I will modify my scoring system. I will still have two scores, one for short term and one for longer term.

Short-term scoring system

The scoring system should work better in the shorter term. For testing this system, I used the above database, but deleted stocks that have been over 8 months old. It is still a small database of about 190 stocks.

The result is different from the above as the time frame has been reduced. Here is the summary.

- The predictability of screens (same as searches) performs about the same as the last monitor. A few screens are better than others. I will not use the under-performing screens with real money.
- The stock grades from several vendors are not a good indicator this time.
- Expected (same as Forward) Earnings Yield (E/P) has been a good indicator.
- Cash Flow is a good indicator (different from the last monitor).
- Fidelity's Equity Summary Score is a good indicator. Finviz has a similar score, but I prefer to use Fidelity's. Fidelity places higher weight on opinions from analysts that have a better prediction on this stock than others. It eliminates some of the conflict of interest between the analysts and the investing banks s/he works for.
- The Short Percentage between 25 and 30 is a good contrary indicator (could be a good chance for a short squeeze). Its value of less than 10 % is a good indicator. The rest of the range is not conclusive.
- Cash / Market Cap, Insider Purchase, P/B, ROE and Dividend stocks (>3%) are not conclusive in this monitor.
- P/S with values less than 0.8 are a good indicator.
- For some reason I do not know why and how to explain: the top 10% of the top-scored stocks did not perform better than the other stocks that pass.
- It happens in both my two scoring systems. Be suspicious of them and it has happened for more than once. However, the stocks that scored in the bottom 10% are consistently poor performers and that's a good indicator.

Section I: Fundamental metrics

3   Mysteries of P/E

If you believe you can make good money by selecting stocks with low P/E ratios alone, think again. If it were that easy, there would be no poor people. However, buying fundamentally sound companies can reduce risk and improve the chances of stock appreciation.

P/E is one of the most misunderstood indicators. To me, it is one of the most useful metrics if used correctly. Earnings are the key to stock appreciation, and the P/E ratio measures its value. For example, imagine paying a million dollars for a hot dog cart in New York City. Even if its earnings increase year after year, you will never recoup your investment because you paid too much for a good business.

The advice to "buy stocks with a P/E below 15 and positive earnings" is not always true. P/E growth (PEG) should also be considered as it reflects the company's future prospects. Many retailers were destroyed by Amazon, and many newspapers were disrupted by Facebook and Google. Which sector would you rather invest in: one that is trending upward or one that is dying, even if it has a better P/E ratio?
Most old books on value investing are based on outdated industries that are no longer applicable in today's market. Read these books, but always ask the question: Is this sector still relevant?

Better Definition

The P/E ratio should be inverted as E/P, which is termed **Earnings Yield**. Earnings Yield is easier to compare and understand. It also handles negative earnings when screening and ranking stocks (comparing stocks with better P/E ratios first). If you sort P/E in ascending order, your ranking will be incorrect for stocks with negative earnings, but it will be correct with E/P.

Earnings Yield is usually compared to a 10-year Treasury bill yield (or 30-year yield) or a CD rate. If a stock has a 5% earnings yield and your one-year CD yields 1%, the stock beats the CD by 4% in absolute terms and is four times better. However, the CD is virtually risk-free (with deposit amount limits in most banks). Earnings Yield is an estimated guess and may not materialize.

Many Ways to Predict E/P
- **Based on the last 12 months**: Project it to the Forward E/P. This is also called the last twelve-month E/P.
- **Based on analysts' educated guesses**: These guesses may not materialize. Based on my experience, forward earnings (expected earnings) usually predict better than the last 12 months' earnings. This is the metric I use most often, and many investing subscriptions provide this Forward P/E (same as Expected P/E) or expected E/P.

I usually don't trust analysts' opinions due to conflicts of interest. However, earnings estimates are an exception.
- **Based on the last month or the last quarter**: The latest information could be better for predictions. However, this method is not suitable for seasonal businesses, such as retail, where most sales occur during the Christmas season.
- **Average Earnings Yield (Avg. EY)**: Besides the Pow PE described later, I take the average of the earnings yield (EY) as:

Avg. EY=EY from the last twelve months+Expected EY+EY from the current month of the prior year3Avg. EY=3EY from the last twelve months+Expected EY+EY from the current month of the prior year

This averages out figures from the past, present, and future. If no one has used this method, I shamelessly claim it as my original idea.

Best E/P May Not Be the Best
A very high E/P could indicate trouble ahead, such as a pending lawsuit, fraud, etc. If you find companies with an E/P over 50%, it means two years' profits could equal the entire cost of the company! I can tell you right away that these companies probably smell fishy unless you believe in free lunches.

However, bargains do exist from time to time due to certain conditions or because Wall Street is wrong about the company. I found one in my year-end screen, and it gave me a huge return. You need to determine whether these are bargains or traps. When the E/P is low (sometimes even negative) but improving rapidly, it could mean big profits for you. Fundamentalists may miss this opportunity in the early stages due to unfavorable E/P, but it could be the most profitable time to buy. Sometimes, it could signal a turnaround.

During a recession, most good companies struggle to promote new products as consumers become thrifty. At the same time, it is usually the best time to develop products if the company has enough cash to finance them. In this case, there will be no alarm even with negative earnings. The only alarm is when a company cannot meet its debt obligations.

Some companies can manipulate earnings through accounting tricks. This can make the current year look good, but it is harder or even impossible to continue the same trick for many years. Always check the footnotes in the financial statements.

E/P and PEG

For value investing, E/P is usually used, and the higher, the better. Be cautious when it is extraordinarily high.

PEG (P/E growth) measures the rate of improvement in the P/E ratio. A PEG of '1' is considered neutral for most investors. When it is below 1, the stock is undervalued, and vice versa.

$$PEG = \frac{P/E}{\text{Earnings Growth Rate}}$$

PEG has a similar problem to P/E when earnings are negative.

Which of the following two stocks would you buy based on their historical earnings yields and earnings growth?
1. A stock with a 10% earnings yield and no earnings growth.
2. A stock with an 8% earnings yield and 50% earnings growth.

If the earnings growth continues, the second stock should yield 12% next year, substantially better than the first stock. This is another reason to use forward earnings rather than historical earnings.

PEG may give a low value for companies that pay high dividends. To correct this:

$$PEG = \frac{P/E}{\text{Earnings Growth Rate} + \text{Dividend Yield}}$$

When the general market favors growth stocks, weigh more on growth metrics, including PEG. I claim no credit for the adjusted PEG.

Fundamental Metrics

E/P is one of the metrics you should use, but not exclusively. If the earnings yield is high but the percentage of debt is also high, then a good bargain may not be as good as it appears.

Some other metrics may not be easily found in financial statements, such as intangibles, insider buying, pension obligations, trade secrets, losing market share, brand name, customer loyalty, etc. It is interesting that the predictive ability of most metrics changes over time.

P/E Variations

There are other P/E variations, such as the Shiller P/E (also known as CAPE and PE10). The Shiller P/E can also be used to track the current market valuation. It is controversial, and its value is easily misinterpreted. Use it as a reference only unless you understand all its issues. I prefer to use a two-year average of the P/E instead of 10 years, as I believe the market changes too much over a decade. Currently, the Shiller P/E does not work as well as it used to, likely due to excessive money printing.

Compare a company's current P/E to its average P/E over the last five years. Also, compare it to the average P/E of companies in the same industry. The average P/E for high-tech companies is different from that of supermarkets, for example. These averages are available from Fidelity.

P/E is more reliable for a group of stocks (e.g., SPY) rather than individual stocks, which have too many other metrics and intangibles to consider. When comparing the total return of an ETF to its corresponding index, add the respective dividends to the index to ensure a fair comparison of total returns. As of this writing, the S&P 500 is paying about a 2% dividend.

EV/EBITDA is another way to measure a company's value. This metric has its advantages and disadvantages compared to P/E. It includes other important data, such as cash and debt. EBITDA/EV is equivalent to E/P, including other mentioned metrics. I prefer to use it over E/P. Some sites do not provide EV/EBITDA if earnings are negative. The disadvantage, in my opinion, is that it does not use expected earnings. This ratio can be found on Yahoo!Finance.

Garbage In, Garbage Out

I do not trust most financial statements from emerging countries, especially from smaller companies. Watch out for fraudulent data. Most metrics can be manipulated. Recently, I had a U.S. stock that lost 18% in one day due to an SEC investigation into its financial data. The announced earnings may not be reflected in the financial statements you find online. Ensure your data is up-to-date by checking the date of the financial statements. Seeking Alpha has transcripts of earnings announcements that can save you a trip to attend the companies' quarterly meetings.

Sector and Entire Market

You can find the value of a sector using the P/E of an ETF for that sector. The same applies to the entire market. For example, use SPY (an ETF that simulates the S&P 500 index). If its P/E is lower than the average (15, in my opinion), the market is likely a good value and a buy signal. This is one of many hints for market timing.

Where to Use P/E

Each highlight below corresponds to one of my books. Click the link for a description of the strategy.

My book on the top-down approach starts with a safe market, then sector analysis, fundamental analysis, intangible analysis, and optionally technical analysis. P/E is one of many metrics in fundamental analysis.

There are many investing styles. In general, fundamental analysis is important when you hold a stock for a longer period.

- **P/E is important in Long-Term Swing, Dividend Investing, Retirees, and Conservative Strategies.**
    - My maximum P/E value is 20, and 25 for tech companies. I ignore it if the company has high potential for appreciation, which could be indicated by insider purchases. However, many unknown companies have had P/E ratios over 50. Tesla once had a P/E over 1,000.
- **P/E is moderately important in Short-Term Swing and Sector Rotation.**
- **P/E is least important in Momentum Strategy and Day Trading.**
- **Be cautious of falling companies when the P/E is low due to investors leaving because of events like major lawsuits.**

Summary
Again, one metric should not dictate the reason to trade a stock. Compare the company's P/E to its industry average and its own five-year average. Additionally, many industries have cycles. If you buy at the peak of an industry cycle, the P/E may mislead you. Besides fundamental analysis, consider intangible analysis and time your entry/exit points using <u>technical analysis</u>. Intangible analysis evaluates information that cannot be summarized into numeric metrics, such as a pending lawsuit.

My observations:

True P/E
"<u>EV/EBITDA</u>" is available on Yahoo!Finance and other sources. The true Earnings Yield (EY) is "1/True P/E". I call it "True" for lack of a better term, as it represents the company's financial situation more accurately. This could be the most important metric for many investors.

EBITDA: <u>https://www.youtube.com/watch?v=C2eoh3X4efM</u>

Earnings can be manipulated. For example, company management can lower the P/E ratio by buying back its stock. In this case, earnings per share (EPS) are boosted, but there is no change in the company's financial fundamentals. True P/E takes into account the reduced cash. EBITDA stands for "Earnings Before Interest, Taxes, Depreciation, and Amortization."

Be cautious when EV or EBITDA is negative. Most likely, you should avoid stocks with a negative EV.
Yahoo!Finance usually leaves EV/EBITDA blank for financial institutions such as banks, loan companies, and REITs. In this case, use forward earnings yield (= 1 / Forward P/E) or Pow Earnings Yield, described next.

I prefer True Yield based on Forward P/E rather than trailing P/E, as it has better predictive power. For example, Apple has a P/E of 21.61, a Forward P/E of 19.46 (both from Finviz), and an Enterprise Value/EBIT of 16.72 (from Yahoo!Finance). The True Yield is 6%

(1/16.72). The True Yield based on Forward P/E is 7% (6% * 21.61/19.48).

Pow P/E

You should use the described "EV/EBITDA," and thus "Pow P/E" can be ignored. However, there are some cases where Pow P/E is better: 1) "EV/EBITDA" may not be available due to reasons such as negative assets, and 2) Use of Forward Earnings instead of earnings based on the last twelve months. The following is an exercise on how I simulate it from Finviz.com using readily available metrics.

I modified P/E to account for cash and debt. I use my last name for this metric to distinguish it from P/E, and it has nothing to do with my ego.

$$\text{Pow P/E} = \frac{P - \text{Cash per Share} + \text{Debt per Share}}{\text{Earnings} - \text{Interest gained per share} - \text{Interest paid per share}}$$

$$\text{Pow Earnings Yield} = \frac{1}{\text{Pow P/E}}$$

Here is a comparison of E/P (Earnings Yield), Expected Earnings Yield (Forward E/P), True Yield (EBITDA/EV), and Pow Earnings Yield, based on Forward (Expected) Earnings as of 10/14/2021.

Metric	CARS	MPAA
Earnings Yield	1%	7%
Expected Earnings Yield	12%	12%
True Yield	13%	11%
Pow Earnings Yield	5%	9%

P/E Is Not Always Important

The following is my test from 1/2/2020 to 10/14/2020. RSP is similar to SPY, except that the stocks in the S&P 500 index are equally weighted. EY (= E/P) is Expected Earnings Yield, and there are no stocks with EY less than 0. DY is Dividend Yield. GPE is the growth of P/E. As in my book, I use annualized returns, and dividends are not included.

This test does not mean much, but it tells us how these metrics behaved during this period. It indicates that **value was not a good metric during this period**, and it may suggest that momentum was better.

Most big winners start as small companies with **high P/E ratios** (from 30 to 100). Many of them have important technologies or systems that could change the world, such as Microsoft, Facebook, Amazon, and Walmart, to name a few. Their sales have increased substantially year after year. In early 2023, P/E for many AI chips, such as Nvidia, was not important when the industry looked rosy, and the Forward P/E was far better than the trailing P/E (based on the last 12 months).

Examples of not depending on low P/Es: Before the 2008 financial crisis, most bank stocks had 10-year low P/Es. After they announced earnings, the P/Es of many surged to over 100, and stock prices suffered losses of more than 80% within 12 months. Bethlehem Steel's stock price, with a P/E of 2 at one time, went to zero. You need to find out why the stock is so cheap through intangible and qualitative analysis.

The following is a rough test with many limitations in the database. However, the conclusion is quite convincing to me, and some results are contrary to common beliefs. For example, I expected higher EY to be better, but that was not the case in this test.

Metric	Ann. Return	Indicator	Comment
RSP 500 All	-2%		
EY (top 10)	-54%	Bad	Contrary
GPE (top 10)	-20%	Bad	Contrary
Select All or top 100.			
DY = 0	16%	Good	
DY (top 100)	-19%	Bad	
DY / 1 and 2	2%		
EY 3 to 4	15%	Good	Second best
EY 2 to 3	6%	Good	Third best
EY 1 to 2	31%	Good	Best
EY 0 to 1	-39%	Bad`	

I use some metrics from a subscription service that are not included here. Two major metrics from this subscription have a return of around 20%. Most subscriptions, including Fidelity (to some extent), provide three composite scores: Total, Fundamental, and Timing. I wish to check the recent predictability of Fidelity's Equity Summary Score if they have a historical database. Most of them exclude delisted or bankrupt companies from their databases.

Link: P/E: https://www.youtube.com/watch?v=4KkTGx2bK_4

4   Fundamental metrics

ROE (Return on Equity)
Return on Equity (ROE = Net Income / Equity) is one of the most important financial indicators to assess how effectively a company's management is performing. However, in recent years, this metric has been overused, leading to a decline in its predictive reliability.

A company's ROE over the last five years can provide insight into how well the stock price withstands major financial downturns and upturns. Comparing a company's ROE to the sector average is a useful way to gauge how well the company is managed relative to its peers. Note that some sectors, such as utilities, typically have lower average ROEs.

Market Cap (Capitalization)
Market Cap = Total Number of Outstanding Shares × Share Price
For beginners, I recommend investing in U.S. stocks with a market cap greater than $800 million. Below is a general classification of market caps, which should be adjusted for inflation over time:

Class	Market Cap (million)
Nano Cap	< $50M
Micro Cap	$50M to $250M
Small Cap	$250M to $1B
Mid Cap	$1B to $10B
Large Cap	$10B to $50B
Mega Cap	> $50B

Generally, the higher the market cap, the lower the risk associated with the stock. Nano Cap and Micro Cap stocks are typically reserved for speculators or company owners.

Small Cap and Mid Cap stocks are suitable for knowledgeable investors, as most institutional investors tend to avoid these, especially Small Cap stocks. Large Cap, Mega Cap, and some Mid Cap stocks are commonly traded by institutional investors and are continuously researched.

My Preferred Metrics:

- **Forward P/E**
- **PEG Ratio**
- **Fidelity's Equity Summary Score**
- **Short % of Outstanding Shares**
- **Free Cash Flow**
- **ROE**
- **Debt Load / Equity**

I also use summarized metrics from various sources. For example, one of my subscription services provides a composite rank for fundamentals and another for momentum. As an illustration, you can check Blue Chip Growth (note: this service is no longer free).

Enter IBM as the stock symbol. As of February 2013, it received a C for Total Grade, D for Quantity Grade, and B for Fundamental Grade. The Total Grade is usually a composite of other grades.

Use these metrics to screen stocks and narrow down your options for further consideration.

Mid, High, and Low Values of Common Metrics

Metric	Mid Range	Low Range	High Range
P/E (last 12 months)	< 10	> 40	< 4
Price / Cash Flow	< 12	> 30	< 4
Price / Sales	< 2.5	> 3	< 0.2
Price / Book	< 2.0	> 4	< 0.2
PEG	< 1.5	> 2	< 0.2

High Range values (low numbers in this table) are generally favorable, but sometimes they may be too good to be true. Low Range values are typically unfavorable.

For example, many internet stocks in 2000 had P/E ratios over 40 (bad), while a neglected bargain stock might have a P/E of 3 (supposedly good). However, such bargains could indicate hidden problems.

In practice, I prefer the Mid Range. For instance, a P/E between 4 and 10 is ideal. Adjust these ranges based on your risk tolerance and current market conditions. If the market is trending upward, you might relax the range to 5 to 12 to find more stocks for evaluation.

These values are based on data from the past 10 years and are used to predict stock performance over a year. Review these ranges every six months to account for current market conditions.

Metrics with High-Range and Mid-Range values tend to offer better predictions for stock price appreciation. Stocks with Low-Range values are statistically more likely to lose money over the next year. However, some favorable metrics, such as ROE, may have high values instead of low values.

The effectiveness of these ranges can change. When the market favors momentum, metrics like PEG and price growth may become better predictors. It's essential to monitor which metrics the market currently favors—Value or Growth—and adjust your strategy accordingly.

Evaluate the performance of each metric every 3 to 6 months and update the range values as needed.

Fundamental metrics typically take longer (6-12 months) to materialize compared to momentum metrics (1 month). The metrics in the table above, except for PEG, are all fundamental metrics. Note that Price-to-Book (P/B) is generally not useful for financial stocks.

Examples of Searching with High-Range Values

Stocks with Low-Range values for most metrics (e.g., a P/E of 40) are often risky. Therefore, focus on stocks with Mid-Range values (e.g., a P/E of 10) and avoid Low-Range values.

Here's an example of selecting stocks with High-Range values for P/E and P/B:
Copy
E > 0 and
P/E < 4 and
P/B < 0.2

E represents earnings per share, and we want the company to be profitable. High-Range values could indicate potential issues, such as pending lawsuits. A P/E of less than 4 is often suspicious, but very small 0companies may be overlooked by the market and could still be solid investments.

Always conduct thorough due diligence before investing. Statistically, stocks with Low-Range values are more likely to lose money over the next year, though there are exceptions. For example, Amazon (AMZN) has historically had a high P/E and P/B, but its focus on market share and infrastructure investment has justified its valuation. Personally, I prefer fundamentally sound companies.

Note: P/B is not a reliable metric for established companies or those with significant intellectual property, such as IBM. Many traditional metrics are outdated as they fail to account for intangible assets like patents and brand value.

Example of a Search for Mid-Range Values

$E > 0$ and
$P/E < 10$ and
$P/E > 4$

This search includes companies with positive earnings and P/E ratios between 4 and 10. You should find many companies within this range. Add additional filters, such as minimum price, market cap, and average volume, to narrow down your results. If you find too few stocks, relax your criteria, and vice versa. If you usually find stocks with a screen but not today, it may indicate that the market is overvalued.

This is the first step in narrowing down stocks for further analysis. Keep in mind that some stocks, like IBM, may have consistently high Price/Book values and should not be excluded based on this metric alone.

Compare a Company's Metrics to Its Sector Averages
Comparing a company's metrics to its sector averages is a powerful way to evaluate its performance. For example, the average P/S ratio for supermarkets is extremely low, so

comparing a supermarket's P/S to other sectors is not meaningful. Similarly, utility companies often require high debt levels to operate.

If the average P/E or other metric for a sector is suddenly lower than its historical average, it could indicate that the sector is out of favor or undervalued.

The table below compares Apple to its sector (Computer) and the Retail sector as of a specific date for illustration. Note that these metrics will change over time.

Metric	Apple	Computer	Retail
P/E	11	19	24
5-Year Average P/E	16	17	15
PEG	0.6	N/A	1.4
Price / Cash Flow	9.4	8.1	9.2
Price / Book	3.3	3.0	3.6
EPS Growth (5-Yr)	62%	45%	11%
Operating Margin	20%	15%	8%
ROE	30%	14%	19%
Debt / Equity	2%	7%	88%
Inventory Turnover	76%	53%	4.55x

Some metrics, such as Debt/Equity, are more relevant to specific sectors. For example, retail companies typically have higher Inventory Turnover compared to computer companies.

Top-Down Approach
1. Assess whether the market is risky.
2. Select the best-performing sector using tools like Finviz.com.
3. Compare the fundamental metrics of major stocks within that sector.

Metrics That May Not Apply
For financial institutions, Price-to-Book (P/B) is often more useful than Price-to-Cash Flow (P/CF). However, the quality of loans is more critical than any metric, as seen during the 2007 financial crisis. For retail companies, Price-to-Sales (P/S) is more important, while expected P/E is crucial for most other sectors.

When you identify a sector as the best-performing, select the top stocks within that sector.

Compare Metrics to Their Five-Year Averages

If a company's five-year average P/E is 20 and its current P/E is 10, it may be undervalued by 100%. Similarly, compare other metrics, such as Debt/Equity, to their historical averages.

Growth Metrics

Growth metrics, such as the growth rates of stock price, sales, and earnings, are essential for growth investors. Even for value investors, earnings growth is critical, as most stocks with substantial gains have shown earnings growth first. If earnings grow while the stock price remains stagnant, the potential for price appreciation increases, and the stock may return to its historical average P/E.

Momentum Metrics

Momentum metrics, such as the rate of stock price increase and trading volume, are part of growth investing. Earnings revisions are particularly important during earnings seasons (typically four times a year).

Fidelity and other services provide composite momentum scores, which may include metrics like SMA-50, quarter-over-quarter sales growth, and recent price appreciation. For momentum strategies, I focus on these metrics and ignore others, as my average holding period is less than 30 days.

Insider Buying

Insiders sell stocks for various reasons, but when they buy shares at market prices, it's worth noting. Insiders have the best knowledge of their company's health and industry trends.

Use sites like Finviz.com or OpenInsider to track insider purchases, focusing on high ratios of Net Total Purchase Value to Market Cap and purchases by multiple insiders. Be cautious if insiders buy stocks shortly after selling a similar amount.

Where to Get Metrics

You can access this information from free or low-cost websites like Finviz.com, your broker's site, AAII, and Fidelity.

For more advanced tools, consider subscription services like Value Line, IBD, Zacks, VectorVest, and Stock Screen 123, which typically cost less than $1,000 per year. Many vendors provide composite metrics, such as value or timing scores, which combine multiple indicators.

Monitor Recent Performance of Metrics
The predictability of metrics can vary depending on market conditions. To identify which metrics are currently effective, evaluate their performance over the last three months and focus on those that perform well. This approach is the basis of my scoring system in the book *Scoring Stocks*.

Why Some Metrics Fail
Despite their widespread use, many investors struggle to achieve consistent success with metrics. Some reasons for this include:

1. Metrics must be monitored for effectiveness in current market conditions.
2. Intangible factors often play a significant role.
3. Popular metrics, like ROE, lose effectiveness when too many investors rely on them.
4. Fundamental metrics require time (at least 6 months) to reflect a stock's value.
5. Data quality issues, especially in emerging markets, can lead to inaccurate metrics.
6. Metrics derived from outdated financial statements may not reflect current conditions.
7. Companies may manipulate metrics, such as P/E and ROE, by taking on excessive debt.

Footnote
1. Stocks are classified into sectors, which are further divided into industries. For simplicity, I use the terms interchangeably here.
2. Amazon (AMZN) is not a value stock by traditional metrics. As of January 2013, its P/E was 157, and its P/B was 15, both falling into the Low-Range category. Despite this, its stock price rose from 256 to256 *to* 270 in January 2013, driven by investor optimism about its market share growth. While it

may be suitable for traders, it is too risky for long-term investors like me.

Afterthoughts
- One popular investment book recommends selecting stocks based solely on ROE. I can save you time and money by telling you that this approach no longer works.
- Delta Air Lines (DAL) has an interesting Debt/Equity ratio of over -1000% due to negative equity. In such cases, consider using Debt/ABS(Equity) for comparison.
- Occasionally, financial data discrepancies arise between sources. Always verify the dates of financial statements, as the company's website typically provides the most up-to-date information.
- The Current Ratio (Current Assets / Current Liabilities) is a useful metric. A ratio below 1 indicates that a company may struggle to meet its short-term obligations.
- Dividend Yield is a valid metric for mature companies but is less relevant for growth companies that reinvest earnings into research and development.
- Finviz.com provides three margin metrics: Profit Margin, Gross Margin, and Operating Margin. I prefer Profit Margin for most companies, though the others may be relevant in specific sectors.
- Enron had millions in profits but negative cash flows, highlighting the importance of cash flow analysis over earnings.
- Insider selling is usually not a cause for concern unless excessive. Insiders often sell shares before a company goes bankrupt.
- Shorting stocks can be challenging, even with strong fundamental arguments. Not every investment will be profitable, but educated decisions should outperform the market in the long run.
- Intrinsic value is a useful concept but is often overlooked due to its complexity. It represents the real value of a company, which may differ from its book value or market cap.

Links:
Income statement: https://www.youtube.com/watch?v=ht-tzwyLPU

The following link provides more info on intrinsic value.
http://en.wikipedia.org/wiki/Intrinsic_value_%28finance%29
https://www.youtube.com/watch?v=l-T-Vyk2txc&authuser=0

5   Finviz's parameters

Stock Metrics and Analysis

Most metrics are described in Finviz (via Help), Investopedia, and/or Wikipedia, as well as in my articles on P/E and fundamental metrics if available. We use these metrics for screening stocks and then evaluating the screened stocks. Most metrics can also be obtained from Yahoo! Finance and Google Finance.

The following are my personal comments on why I believe some metrics are more important than others. Personally, I divide metrics into **fundamental** and **technical** categories, which are more relevant for long-term and short-term investors, respectively.

Comparing Ratios
Compare the ratios to companies in the same sector (industry) and also to their averages over the last few years (preferably five years). This information can be obtained from many websites, including Fidelity.

Using Finviz.com
From your browser, enter **Finviz.com**. Enter a stock symbol (I used **ABEO** for this discussion). A chart will be displayed with prices and volumes for the last eleven months. SMAs (Simple Moving Averages) are sometimes displayed along with other technical indicators. Intraday, Daily, and Weekly options are available for day traders, short-term traders, and long-term traders, respectively. I prefer using the **Candle -- Advanced** option for drawing charts.

Besides the chart and the metrics described next, Finviz provides information on what the company does, analysts' recommendations (I prefer Fidelity's Equity Summary Score), insider trading, and articles that are useful for qualitative analysis. Many free websites, such as Yahoo! Finance, also provide a list of articles about the company.

Financial Highlights and Statements
These materials are essential for in-depth analysis and were more critical decades ago when most financial ratios were not pre-calculated. They are still important for investors with a good understanding of financial accounting. The current version of Finviz

includes basic balance sheets, income statements, and cash flow statements for the trailing twelve months (TTM) and the last two years. Click on the following YouTube links for more details:

- **Balance Sheet**: https://www.youtube.com/watch?v=DMv9JC_K37Y
- **Income Statement**: https://www.youtube.com/watch?v=0-_AvwZablQ
- **Cash Flow Statement**: https://www.youtube.com/watch?v=hMBN6yTIDb0

Insider Trading
A section on **Insider Trading** is also included. Do not be alarmed when insiders sell small quantities of stock. However, large purchases (e.g., insider transactions exceeding 5% of shares) at prices close to the market price could be favorable news.

Key Metrics in Finviz
The following metrics are roughly based on the flow of Finviz from top to bottom and left to right. I skip metrics that I believe are less important. You can hover your cursor over a metric to retrieve its description from Finviz or via Finviz's Help. Some metrics are left blank to indicate they are not applicable (e.g., zero, negative, or not available).

For example, the Debt/Equity ratio for **YRCW** in January 2019 was blank due to its negative equity. From Yahoo! Finance at the time of writing, YRCW had a total debt of $888 million.

Index
Most of us trade stocks listed on the three major U.S. exchanges. Stocks listed over-the-counter (OTC) are generally too risky for most investors. Avoid stocks listed on local or foreign exchanges unless you are an expert or have insider knowledge (not illegal). I screen stocks and ignore those not listed on the Dow, NASDAQ, or AMEX. Other screeners may allow you to select a group of exchanges.

Market Cap (MC)
To me, stocks with a market cap below $50 million are risky, even though they could be very profitable. Ensure the average trading volume is at least 10,000 shares, or your order is less than 1% of the average volume. Some small-cap stocks are controlled by their

owners and have low trading volumes, making them difficult to trade.

Float = Outstanding Shares - Insider Shares
Usually, float does not matter as it is typically the same as outstanding shares. However, it is important for small companies with large insider ownership. Most owners of such companies do not want to sell their family businesses, reducing the chance of acquisition. In such cases, you may have to hold the stock for a long time or sell it at an unfavorable price.

Forward P/E
If **Forward P/E** (a.k.a. Expected P/E) is not provided, use the **Trailing P/E**, which is based on the last 12 months (TTM). Alternatively, calculate the earnings (E) by using the earnings from P/E and multiplying it by the company's growth rate. Note that this may not be seasonally adjusted. I prefer using Forward P/E as it provides better predictability. Successful investing often depends on correctly predicting future earnings.

Finviz leaves the P/E blank if earnings are negative. In such cases, I check Yahoo! Finance's **EV/EBITDA**, which also considers taxes, cash, and interest. The blank condition also occurs in other metrics, such as when assets are negative (very rare).

Earnings Yield = E/P.
I call it **True Earnings Yield** for **EBITDA/EV**. It is easier to understand. Compare Earnings Yield or True Yield to the annual dividend yield of a 10-year Treasury bond. However, with low interest rates in 2021, skip this comparison for this year.

E/P is easier for screening and sorting stocks. If you use P/E instead of E/P, you need to screen or sort stocks with the clause "P/E > 0". When the P/E is less than 5, be cautious, as there may be a reason why it is so low. Many companies that eventually go bankrupt had low P/Es at one point before their stock prices collapsed.

Compare the P/E or Forward P/E to the average P/E for the sector (e.g., high tech) and its five-year average, available from Fidelity.com. Some sectors, like technology, typically have high P/Es (e.g., 25). If the sector is cyclical, earnings could be affected.

Do not rely solely on P/E to determine a stock's value. Other metrics, such as PEG, P/B, and Debt/Equity, are also important.

When a company's prospects are strong, such as Tesla in 2020, ignore the P/E. Investors are betting on the future. Do not short these high-growth stocks.

Cash per Share

This metric is used to calculate **Pow P/E** and **Pow EY** when EV/EBITDA is not available. For example, if a stock is priced at \$10 and has \$10 cash per share with no debt (i.e., Debt/Equity = 0), it is likely underpriced, as you could theoretically acquire the entire company for free. Investigate why the price is so low—it could be market neglect or a serious event like a major lawsuit. **P/C** (Price-to-Cash) is a better choice than Cash per Share; the lower the better.

Dividend %

This metric is useful for income investors. The payout ratio should not exceed 30%, except for mature companies. Most growth and tech companies reinvest profits into research and development, so they do not pay dividends.

Recommendations (Recs)

It is no longer available. If it is available again, select stocks with a recommendation score of 1 or 2. Do not base your stock selection solely on this metric, as many bad recommendations have led to significant losses. Use Fidelity's **Equity Summary Score** instead.

PEG Ratio

The **PEG Ratio** measures the growth of P/E and is a growth metric (others include Sales Growth Q/Q and Earnings Growth Q/Q). It is similar to P/E but takes the expected earnings growth rate into account.

A lower PEG is better as long as earnings are positive. If earnings are negative, the reverse is true. This is a limitation of using P/E and PEG, which is why I recommend **Earnings Yield (EY)** and **Earnings Yield Growth (EYG)**. The chance of stock appreciation is high when the PEG is less than 1.

If two companies have the same P/E, the one with a better PEG ratio is preferable. Similarly, if two companies have the same E/P, the one with higher Earnings Growth (EPS Q/Q) is better.

Price-to-Book (P/B)
Book value (Total Assets - Total Liabilities) may not include intangible assets like patents. Do not rely on it entirely, just as with ROE and other metrics based on book value. Negative equity is possible when Total Liabilities exceed Total Assets.

This metric is outdated for most mature companies, as their value now includes intangible assets like patents, management quality, brand names, market share, and customer base. Some assets, like gold mines and real estate, can be easily valued. For example, when gold prices fall, a company's P/B could drop below 1, making it a potential buy—unless the downward trend continues.

Price-to-Sales (P/S)
If two companies are unprofitable, the P/S ratio could be more useful. Retail companies like Walmart have very different P/S ratios compared to research companies. This metric is only meaningful when comparing stocks within the same or related sectors.

Price-to-Free Cash Flow (P/FCF)
I prefer this metric to be greater than 0 and less than 50 for value investors. Most metrics can be manipulated, but not this one. It is a key metric for avoiding bankrupt companies.

Sales Growth Q/Q
This metric reduces seasonal deviations. For example, retail sales during the Christmas season should be compared to the same season in the prior year.

Earnings Growth Q/Q
Similar to Sales Growth Q/Q, I prefer Earnings Growth over Sales Growth. Both are growth metrics. When a company discontinues unprofitable products, its Sales Growth Q/Q may decline, but its Earnings Growth Q/Q could increase. In 2000, many internet companies had strong Sales Growth Q/Q but negative Earnings Growth Q/Q.

Quarter-over-quarter (Q/Q) comparisons eliminate seasonal variations. I prefer both Sales Growth Q/Q and Earnings Growth Q/Q to increase. If Earnings Growth Q/Q increases significantly more than Sales Growth Q/Q, it could indicate temporary factors, such as a spike in oil prices for an oil company.

When a company buys back its own shares, EPS can be misleading, as earnings (E) remain fixed while the number of shares decreases. In most cases, the company's fundamentals have not changed.

In 2021, many energy stocks had incredible Earnings Growth Q/Q, and their Forward P/E ratios were better than their Trailing P/E ratios. These could be momentum plays unless their growth is sustainable.

Insider Transactions
Positive insider transactions are favorable. However, they can sometimes be misleading. Scroll to the end of the screen for more details. If the transactions are outdated (e.g., three months old) or involve purchases following similar sales, they are less significant. Insiders know their company better than outsiders.

Institutional Transactions
This metric is also important, as institutional investors can move the market. However, most institutional investors avoid small-cap stocks, so this metric is less relevant for them.

Insider Ownership, Shares Outstanding, and Float
These metrics determine the number of shares available for trading. Stocks with low float and high insider ownership limit trading and should generally be avoided. Compare your trade size to the stock's average trading volume.

Profit Margin
I prefer **Profit Margin** over **Gross Margin** and **Operating Margin**, as it includes interest expenses and taxes. For example, software companies have high Gross Margins, as they exclude development, support, and marketing costs. Retail stores, on the other hand, have low Gross Margins. It is best to compare companies within the same industry.

Short Float
I prefer a Short Float of less than 10%. If it exceeds 10%, short sellers may have identified issues with the company. If it exceeds 25%, check the company's fundamentals and any significant events, such as major lawsuits. If the fundamentals are strong, consider buying

the stock, anticipating a potential short squeeze. This strategy is risky but has proven profitable in some of my trades.

Technical Metrics: SMA-20, SMA-50, and SMA-200
Finviz expresses these moving averages as percentages. If all are positive, the trend is upward. SMA-20 and SMA-50 are short-term trend indicators, while SMA-200 is a long-term trend indicator. Short-term swing traders should focus on short-term trends, while long-term investors should consider long-term trends.

For no need for charting, I modified the **Golden Cross** (SMA-20 crossing above SMA-50) and **Death Cross** (SMA-20 crossing below SMA-50) as buy and sell signals, respectively.

Relative Strength Index (RSI-14)
If RSI is above 65%, the stock is overbought and may reverse. If it is below 30%, the stock is oversold and may rebound. Some traders use thresholds of 70% and 30%. Use RSI as a reference, but note that many stocks making new highs remain overbought for extended periods. I recommend using trailing stops to protect profits on rising stocks.

Beta
A stock with a high Beta is more volatile. Higher Beta stocks are suitable for short-term traders. A Beta of 1 means the stock moves with the market, while a Beta above 1 indicates higher volatility. For volatile stocks, set wider stop-loss levels (e.g., 15% instead of 10%).

Performance (Perf)
If a stock has lost more than 50% of its value, it could be a candidate for bottom fishing—or it could be heading toward bankruptcy. Conduct thorough research before buying such risky stocks.

Return on Equity (ROE)
ROE measures management performance. Institutional ownership (except for small companies) and insider ownership reflect confidence in the company and its sector.

ROE = Net Income / Average Shareholder's Equity
According to Investopedia, a normal ROE for utilities is around 10%, while high-tech companies should aim for 15%. Compare this ratio to industry peers using data from Fidelity and other sources.

Avoiding Bankrupt Companies

Avoid companies at risk of bankruptcy at all costs. Metrics like Debt/Equity, P/FCF, Cash per Share, P/B, Profit Margin, Forward P/E, Short Float, RSI-14, SMA-20, and SMA-50 can provide warning signs. Summarize all information and consider other factors, such as obsolete products or pending generic drug approvals. Read articles available on Finviz and other sites.

Earnings Date

Avoid trading stocks a week before their earnings date (available on Finviz). It is rare to make significant profits if earnings exceed expectations, as the stock price often reflects anticipated results. Conversely, disappointing earnings can cause significant price declines.

Additional Useful Information

Equity

Equity = Total Assets - Total Liabilities. When equity is negative, many metrics based on equity (e.g., P/B, Debt/Equity) are not displayed. For example, on May 5, 2022, **TUP** had equity of -$207 million (from Finviz's balance sheet as of December 25, 2021). When equity is zero or negative, related metrics like P/B, Debt/Equity, and EV/EBITDA may be blank or null.

However, a P/E of less than 4 could indicate a buying opportunity unless there are significant underlying issues. Some large companies had low P/Es before going bankrupt.

Earnings Date

Earnings announcements, typically quarterly, can cause significant stock price fluctuations (e.g., 10%).

Price Chart

The price chart includes features like resistance lines and technical indicators such as double tops (bearish) and double bottoms (bullish).

Company Description

The description under the stock symbol provides a brief overview of the company's sector, industry, and country of registration. Invest in stocks within sectors that are trending upward. For example, according to Finviz, Apple is in the Consumer Goods sector and the Electronic Equipment industry.

Avoid foreign stocks unless they are listed on U.S. exchanges or headquartered in the U.S. Foreign stocks carry additional risks, such as currency fluctuations, lack of regulation, and political instability (e.g., Russia in 2022 and China in 2021). Some foreign stocks may also impose additional taxes on dividends.

Articles on the Company
Articles provide qualitative analysis and insights into the company.

Insider Trading
Pay attention to insider purchases at market prices. Use common sense when interpreting insider transactions.

Intrinsic Value
Many websites (most requiring subscriptions) calculate intrinsic value. Use it as a reference, but evaluate the stock yourself. Buy when the intrinsic value is below the stock price and sell when it is above. This aligns with the "buy low, sell high" principle. However, consider other intangible factors. Stocks like Tesla and Amazon had low intrinsic values but continued to rise.

Other Important Sites

Yahoo! Finance
From the **Statistics** tab, you can find **Enterprise Value / EBITDA**. I call it **True Yield** when inverted to **EBITDA / Enterprise Value**. If unavailable, use **Earnings Yield**. In my spreadsheet:

=IF(Earnings Yield = "", True Yield, Earnings Yield)

Fidelity
Under the **Stock, Statistics,** and **More** tabs, you can compare the P/E to the five-year average using spreadsheets.
Cheaper By Historically =IF(PE="","",(Avg. of 5-year PE - PE)/Avg. of 5-year PE)

Compare the P/E to industry peers:

Cheaper By To the Peers =IF(PE="","",(Industry PE - PE)/Industry PE)

Your Broker's Website
Your broker's website should have plenty of tools for stock analysis. As of December 2018, Fidelity offers extensive research for free with no position restrictions. Some useful metrics include:

- **Equity Summary Score**: A score of 7 or higher (8 for conservative investors) indicates a potentially good buy. Avoid stocks with scores of 3 or below. Scores between 4 and 6 could be turnaround candidates if supported by strong earnings growth or positive news.
- **Five-Year Averages**: These are good benchmarks. For example, in December 2018, **C** had a P/E of 9, compared to its five-year average of 14, making it a value buy.

Other Sources
If you have access to other sources (most require subscriptions), avoid stocks with failing grades. Exceptions include new positive developments or increased insider purchases.

Vendor	Grade	Fail
Fidelity	Equity Summary Score	< 7
IBD	Composite Grade	< 50
Value Line	Projected 3-5 Year Return	< 3%
Zacks	Rank	5
VectorVest	VST	< 0.7

You may find Value Line and IBD in your local library. Start with free stock reports from your broker. Finviz and Seeking Alpha offer articles on stocks and earnings conferences, which can provide valuable insights.

Guru Analysis
It is helpful to know how investment gurus rate stocks. **GuruFocus** is a good source but requires a subscription. **NASDAQ** offers a simplified version. Visit Nasdaq.com, select "Investing," then "Guru Screeners," and enter a stock symbol like **THO**. You will see how 10 or so gurus evaluate the stock. Click "Detailed Analysis" for each guru's perspective.

Quick and Dirty Stock Evaluation

Sometimes, you need to evaluate a stock quickly due to market developments or to narrow down a list of screened stocks. Here are two methods:

Simplest Way to Evaluate Stocks
This method takes a few minutes. Open Finviz.com and enter the stock symbol.

Using **SWKS** on June 10, 2016, as an example:
- **Forward P/E**: ~11 (fine between 3 and 25)
- **Debt/Equity**: 0 (fine if less than 0.5)
- **ROE**: 30% (fine if greater than 5%)
- **P/PCF**: 31 (fine if not negative)

Also, check **Market Cap**, **Average Volume**, **Dividend**, **Short Float** (fine between 0% and 10%), **Country**, and **Industry**. Based on these metrics, **SWKS** is a buy.

If you have more time, check:
- **Recommendations**: Fine if less than 2.5
- **P/B**: Fine between 0.5 and 4
- **Sales Growth Q/Q**: Fine if not negative
- **Earnings Growth Q/Q**: Fine if not negative
- **Cash per Share**: Compare to Debt per Share
- **Profit Margin**: Fine if greater than 5%

Read articles about the stock for additional insights.

5-Minute Stock Evaluation
This method is even quicker but less thorough. I recommend spending more time researching stocks.
1. Open Finviz.com and enter the stock or ETF symbol. Look at the number of red metrics. If there are more reds than greens, the stock is likely not a good buy.
2. Check Fidelity's **Equity Summary Score**. A score above 8 is favorable.
3. If time allows, check:
    - **Forward P/E**: E > 0 and P/E < 20
    - **Debt/Equity**: < 50%
    - **P/FCF**: Not in the red

4. Replace Forward P/E with **True P/E** (EV/EBITDA) if possible, available from Yahoo! Finance.
5. Check **SMA-20** (or SMA-50 for longer holding periods). If SMA-20 is > 10%, the stock is trending upward.
6. Positive **Insider Transactions** are favorable.
7. Be cautious with foreign stocks and low-volume stocks.
8. If most metrics are positive, the stock is likely a buy. However, nothing is 100% certain.

Links

PEG: http://en.wikipedia.org/wiki/PEG_ratio
Short %: http://www.investopedia.com/university/shortselling/shortselling1.asp#axzz2LNDvpemo
Openinsider: http://www.openinsider.com/
Finviz: http://Finviz.com/
terms: http://www.Finviz.com/help/screener.ashx
Insider Cow: http://www.insidercow.com/
Current Ratio: http://en.wikipedia.org/wiki/Current_ratio
Cash Flow: https://www.youtube.com/watch?v=1v8hRZ36--c
How to find quality stocks.
http://seekingalpha.com/article/2381395-how-to-identify-quality-stocks-and-is-there-really-alpha-to-be-had
Over-priced stock:
https://www.youtube.com/watch?v=VeMr0n4pvtM:
Outperform the market
https://www.youtube.com/watch?v=3DdY0JdUilM

Reading financial sheet.
Balance sheet: https://www.youtube.com/watch?v=DZjU0CHKyV4
Earnings report: https://www.youtube.com/watch?v=lte4l_y08Gg

---

https://www.youtube.com/watch?v=DMv9JC_K37Y&t=954s
https://www.youtube.com/watch?v=8NelYFn07jg
Intrinsic Value: https://www.youtube.com/watch?v=I-T-Vyk2txc

More info from Fidelity

Additional Metrics from Fidelity
In addition to Finviz, I also obtain **EV/EBITDA** (Enterprise Value to Earnings Before Interest, Taxes, Depreciation, and Amortization) from **Yahoo! Finance** under the **Statistics** tab. This section will describe more metrics available on **Fidelity**, as well as how to use

them effectively. Note that some metrics may overlap across Finviz, Yahoo! Finance, and Fidelity.

Navigating Fidelity
To begin, start from the **"News & Research"** tab on Fidelity's platform. Here, you can access:
- **"Markets & Sectors"**: Provides an overview of market trends and sector performance, along with related articles and insights.
- **"Viewpoints: Market Sense"**: Offers market analysis and perspectives to help you make informed decisions.

For a visual guide, you can watch this YouTube video: Fidelity Overview.
From the **"News & Research"** tab, you can also access Fidelity's **Screener**, **CDs**, and **Stock** tools.

These tools are invaluable for building an income stream or creating a **CD ladder** based on information from the **"Fixed Income, Bonds, and CDs"** section. For beginners or investors with limited time, **ETFs** (Exchange-Traded Funds) are highly recommended.

Stock Analysis on Fidelity
The **"Stocks"** section on Fidelity provides a wealth of information. The **Home** page offers general market insights and stock-related data. Explore each feature to familiarize yourself with the tools available.

To illustrate, let's use **AAPL (Apple Inc.)** as an example. Enter the stock symbol in the search bar, and you'll find detailed information about the company.

One particularly useful metric is the **Equity Summary Score**, which I find helpful for evaluating stocks. The **5-year P/E ratio**, which was previously located in the main stock overview, has been moved to the **"Statistics"** and **"More"** sections.

Analysis and Sentiment
Fidelity's **"Analysis and Sentiment"** tools help determine whether a stock is **undervalued** (ideal for long-term holding) or has **short-term sentiment** (useful for short-term trading). These tools provide insights into market sentiment and valuation metrics, helping you decide whether to buy, hold, or sell a stock. Currently, the short-

term score, useful for screening momentum stocks, has been eliminated.

Analyst Opinions & Reports
The **"Analyst Opinions & Reports"** section typically includes at least two reports, often more. It's essential to read these reports before making any investment decisions.

Start with reports that have a high **StarMine Relative Accuracy** score, as these are generally more reliable. Some reports also provide historical data, including more than five years of specific metrics. Additionally, you can access the company's **Balance Sheet** and **Income Statement** for a deeper dive into its financial health.

For More Information
For additional guidance on using Fidelity's tools, search for tutorials on **YouTube**. There are many videos available that walk you through the platform's features and how to make the most of them.

Section II: Beyond fundamentals

Buy stocks based on appreciation potential, not based on when and what you traded the stock for.

6   Intangibles

I assign a score to each stock I evaluate. Occasionally, some stocks with poor scores deliver great returns, and vice versa. However, in general, the scoring system works effectively. It has been statistically proven and validated repeatedly through my limited data.

I typically stick with high-score stocks, though there are exceptions. Occasionally, I adjust my scoring system to adapt to current market conditions. For example, during the market bottom and early recovery phases of the market cycle, value stocks tend to outperform momentum or growth stocks. Here are some of my recent experiences and strategies:

- **Increasing Stake in High-Score Stocks**: I often double or even triple my investment in stocks with high scores. Over the long term, these stocks consistently outperform the average, with only minor exceptions. In addition to the score, I also consider the intangibles discussed in this article.
- **Caution with Outrageous Metrics**: Be wary of stocks with extreme metrics, such as a P/E ratio of 4 or less. These could indicate underlying issues like pending lawsuits, expiring patents, or other hidden problems. Similarly, be cautious with stocks in the top 5% of scores, as my data shows they often underperform the average. Their issues may not yet be reflected in the financial statements.
- **Technology and Patents**: For tech companies, the value of their technology and patents cannot be ignored, even if their P/E ratios are high. I set a higher P/E limit of 25 for tech stocks, compared to 20 for others. The value of a company's technology and patents is not captured in fundamental metrics but can sometimes be inferred from insider purchases at market prices.

For example, **IDCC** surged about 40% in two days due to rumors that Google or Apple was bidding for its mobile technology. Charts often flag such events, but for non-chartists, the **SMA-20%** from Finviz.com can provide late but useful signals.

- **Acquisitions During Market Bottoms**: More acquisitions occur during market bottoms and early recovery phases. Companies with valuable technologies become bargains, and larger firms, especially in the same sector, understand their value better than most investors. These potential acquisition targets are not always reflected in their scores. When corporations have ample cash or access to cheap credit, they seek smaller companies with valuable intangible assets like technology, customer base, or market share.

    The periods of 2009-2012 and 2003 were ideal for such investments, and I had at least one stock in each period that appreciated significantly.

- **Overpriced Growth Stocks**: On the flip side, companies like **Netflix**, **Chipotle** (in early 2012), and **Amazon** (in early 2013) were overpriced by any measure. However, these companies were investing heavily in their future, making it difficult for short sellers to profit. When a stock's P/E exceeds 40, exercise caution. While some companies may justify high valuations, most do not. Avoid following the herd and conduct thorough due diligence.

Use the **reward/risk ratio** to guide decisions. For example, if a stock has an equal chance of rising 50% or falling 25%, it is a buy. The reverse would indicate a sell.

- **Unpredictable Events**: Retail investors often cannot anticipate certain events until they occur. For instance, **ATSC** dropped 15% after losing its second primary customer. Fundamental analysis cannot predict such events, and charts often signal them too late unless monitored continuously.
- **Earnings Misses**: After a rapid rise, **TZOO** plunged due to missing negligible earnings expectations. It appears the stock's previous gains had already priced in perfect earnings growth.

I don't understand why a company loses 10% of its market cap for missing earnings by 1%. This could be driven by institutional investors. Evaluate the stock before acting, as going against institutional moves can be profitable for the right stocks. Avoid trading before earnings announcements (typically four times a year for most stocks).

- **Intangibles Not in Financial Statements**: Factors like industry outlook, patents, goodwill, market share, competition, product margins, management quality, pending lawsuits, potential acquisitions, pension obligations, and advertising icons are not easily found in financial statements. This is why it's essential to read articles about stocks on your buy list or in your portfolio.
- **Fraudulent or Manipulated Data**: I am cautious with small companies in emerging markets due to the risk of fraudulent or manipulated financial data. Check company names, especially foreign ones, ADRs, and headquarters addresses (available in most investing sites).

Earnings can be manipulated through accounting tricks. A sudden jump in earnings may not be as positive as it seems. Always check the footnotes in financial statements. I usually skip detailed financial analysis unless I'm considering a significant investment, as my time is limited.

- **Cash Flow**: Cash flow is harder to manipulate and provides insight into a company's survival prospects. However, in my tests, it has not been a consistent predictor of stock performance, though it is a critical red flag for companies nearing bankruptcy.
- **Red Flags**: Repeated one-time, non-recurring, and extraordinary charges are red flags.
- **Overcompensated CEOs**: Avoid companies where CEOs are overcompensated. For example, as of July 2013, **Activision's** CEO raised his salary by over 600% while the stock lost double-digit value.
- **Value Stocks**: Understand why a stock has become a value stock (i.e., fewer investors want to own it), even if it appears fundamentally sound. For example, a supplier to **Apple** might decline due to Apple's falling sales or a switch to alternative suppliers. Technology companies constantly innovate, and a turnaround could occur within a year with better products.
- **Leadership Changes**: The resignation of a CEO or CFO, coupled with heavy insider selling, is not a good sign.

For more insights, watch this video: CEO Compensation and Stock Performance.

Conclusion

Buying a stock is an educated guess that its price will rise. Fundamentals don't always work, but they do most of the time:

1. **Value Stocks Require Patience**: When buying a value stock, you're swimming against the tide. It often takes more than six months for the market to recognize its value. The exception is during the Early Recovery phase of the market cycle, where value stocks can deliver faster and larger returns.
2. **Misleading Metrics**: Some metrics, like book value, can be misleading for established companies like **IBM**. Intangible assets, such as brand image, are not reflected in financial statements.
3. **Market Irrationality**: The market is not always rational.

Afterthoughts

- **Brand Names**: Brand names of large companies are among the most important intangibles. Here's a strategy for buying big companies in a down market. It has been proven to work, but don't buy these companies without analysis.
- **Reputation**: A company's reputation takes years to build but can be destroyed by a single incident, as seen with **GM's** delayed recall of faulty ignition switches.

#Filler: Carrie Fisher, another sad American story

Unless drug addiction is part of the culture now as evidenced from the legalization of certain drugs, we're in a permissive society! Brits pushed opium as a nation when they had nothing better to trade. Opium killed millions of Chinese and bankrupted China. When we do not learn from history, we will repeat history. It is another sad story of fame and money and then losing it all. I bet she would be happier in a normal life instead of being born in a privileged class. Same can be said for many celebrities such as Presley, Houston and her daughter. RIP.

7 Qualitative analysis

Qualitative analysis is the final step in evaluating a stock fundamentally, followed by technical analysis to determine entry and exit points. The market is not always rational and can be influenced by factors like easy credit or liquidity.

Where Quantitative Analysis Fails
Some high-score stocks fail, while some low-score stocks succeed. However, the scoring system works statistically for the majority of my stocks.

Reasons Low-Score Stocks Perform:
1. **Oversold Conditions**: Institutional investors (fund and pension managers) often dump stocks first, followed by retail investors. They may buy back these stocks when prices reach a certain range. Technical indicators like **RSI(14)** (available on Finviz) can help identify oversold stocks.
2. **Price Declines Improve Metrics**: Falling stock prices improve metrics like P/E and P/Sales, but the overall trend remains negative. An improving Forward P/E can be a positive signal.
3. **Turnaround Potential**: A company may have resolved its issues or benefited from market changes. New management, like Steve Jobs' return to **Apple**, can drive profitability.
4. **Insider Purchases**: Increased insider buying can signal positive developments not yet reflected in financial statements, such as resolved lawsuits, new products, or large orders.
5. **Hidden Strengths**: Insiders may hide positive developments to buy more shares at lower prices.

Reasons High-Score Stocks Plunge:
1. **Peak Fundamentals**: Stocks may reach their maximum potential and have no room to grow further. This is especially true when timing ratings are at their highest.
2. **Profit-Taking**: Investors may sell after a stock reaches its target price.
3. **Sector Rotation**: Institutional investors may shift funds to other sectors or stocks with better growth potential.

4. **Deteriorating Outlook**: The company, sector, or market outlook may be worsening. Stocks with P/E ratios below 5 often have underlying issues.
5. **Price Manipulation**: Stocks may be subject to pump-and-dump schemes. Shorting is risky but can be profitable for experienced investors.
6. **Negative Events**: New lawsuits, competing products, or canceled orders can hurt stock prices.
7. **Analyst Downgrades**: Downgrades can signal issues like product defects, regulatory violations, or accounting fraud.
8. **Earnings Misses**: Failing to meet earnings expectations can lead to sharp declines.

Qualitative Analysis

After quantitative and intangible analysis, conduct qualitative analysis to assess a company's prospects. Check the date of articles and watch for hidden agendas. Be cautious of "pump-and-dump" schemes, especially with small companies.

Sources for Qualitative Analysis:
1. **Seeking Alpha**: Search for articles on the company. Paid memberships may be required for access.
2. **Broker Research Reports**: Some brokers provide detailed research reports. Consider opening an account with a broker that offers this service.
3. **Yahoo! Finance Boards**: While most comments are noise, occasional insights can be valuable, especially for small companies.
4. **Company Financial Statements**: Review the most recent statements available on the company's website.
5. **10-K Filings**: Access these from the SEC's EDGAR database (www.sec.gov/edgar). Look for new products, competition, key customers, order backlogs, R&D, and pending lawsuits.
6. **Sector and Company Outlook**: Assess the outlook for the company's sector and its competitive position.
7. **Competitor Analysis**: Evaluate the company's competitors.
8. **Management Quality**: Avoid companies with poor management. For example, **J.C. Penney's** turnaround efforts failed, leading to bankruptcy in 2020.
9. **Business Model**: Evaluate whether the business model makes sense. For example:
    - **Razor-and-Blade Model**: Giving away razors to sell blades is a proven strategy.
    - **Supermarkets**: Lowering prices on common items while profiting from less price-sensitive products like meat and seafood.

- **Barnes & Noble**: A business model reliant on free loaders (e.g., people using stores for air conditioning) is unsustainable.
- **Market dumping** works to capture the market. Microsoft used to do it with their new Office and Mail products that could not compete with the established products at the time. Google is following the same model to dump its equivalent products to compete with Office. Now, Microsoft is taking a dose of the same medicine. As of 2015, Google is not winning.

8 Manipulators and bankruptcy

Avoiding bankruptcies and significant stock value losses can substantially improve our portfolio. Some companies make poor decisions, such as Enron's disastrous bets on energy futures, leading to their downfall. Below are key indicators of potential trouble:

Warning Signs to Watch For:
1. **Foreign Companies**: Investing in small companies from developing countries, such as China, Ireland, and Israel, has not been particularly successful for me. However, as of 2019, many large Chinese companies have been performing well.
2. **P/E Ratio**: If a company's Price-to-Earnings (P/E) ratio appears too good to be true, investigate why. Conversely, avoid companies with excessively poor P/E ratios.
3. **P/PFC Ratio**: The Price-to-Free-Cash-Flow (P/PFC) ratio should be between 0 and 50. Even with healthy cash flow, a company may struggle to service excessive debt. Always compare cash flow to the Debt/Equity ratio.
4. **Altman Z-Score**: A Z-Score above 3 is preferable, as it indicates a low risk of bankruptcy. However, note that the Z-Score is not designed for financial sector companies. The Z-Score is calculated using the following metrics:
   - Working Capital / Total Assets (A)
   - Retained Earnings / Total Assets (B)
   - Earnings Before Interest & Taxes / Total Assets (C)
   - Market Cap / Total Liabilities (D)
   - Sales / Total Assets (E)

   Formula: $Z\text{-Score} = 1.2A + 1.4B + 3.3C + 0.6D + E$
5. **Beneish M-Score**: A score below -2.22 suggests that earnings are not being manipulated. Both Z-Score and M-Score are available on GuruFocus.com for a fee.
6. **Bond Ratings**: Avoid companies with bond ratings below B.

7. **Government Regulations**: Be cautious of new regulations, such as the removal of tax credits for solar panels, which can negatively impact certain industries.
8. **Extraordinary Profits**: Be wary of companies reporting unusually high profits, such as Timber Liquidators or many banks during the 2007-2008 financial crisis.
9. **Accounting Manipulation**: Watch for red flags like excessive stock buybacks to inflate Earnings per Share (EPS), excessive loans to executives, speculative bets on futures (e.g., Enron), frequent one-time charges, or revisions to previous earnings.
10. **Thinly-Traded Stocks**: Avoid stocks with low trading volumes, especially those predominantly owned by a small group of individuals.

The most reliable source for identifying these issues is the company's current financial statements. If something in the statements is unclear, proceed with caution.

Portfolio Management:
To minimize losses, consistently monitor your stock holdings and consider using stop-loss orders to sell before significant value erosion occurs. I recommend maintaining a focused portfolio of around 10 stocks, depending on the time you can dedicate to investing. For example, I hold approximately 10 stocks with larger investments and about 100 smaller positions. Naturally, I spend more time monitoring the 10 core stocks than the rest.

Mergers

Mergers can be beneficial for the involved companies, as they often eliminate redundant functions like payroll administration and overlapping research efforts. Typically, the acquired company experiences a significant appreciation in value. I use a screening process to identify potential acquisition targets, particularly during the "Early Recovery" phase of the market cycle, when undervalued stocks are more prevalent. Large companies often recognize the value in these beaten-down stocks.

Before investing, I conduct an intangible analysis focusing on factors not reflected in financial statements or easily quantifiable. These include:
- Patents and technologies
- Research and development
- Customer base and brand reputation
- Barriers to entry

- Distribution channels
- Competitive landscape
- Product lifecycle
- Management quality
- Pension obligations

For example, in 2003, I invested in a software company later acquired by IBM, more than doubling my investment. During the 2008 cycle, I bought ALU at $1 and sold it for a $401 and sold it for a $403 per share. Patience is key in such scenarios.

However, be cautious: companies targeted for acquisition may manipulate their financial statements to appear more attractive. For instance, a Chinese company misled Caterpillar, resulting in significant losses for the latter. Even large corporations can be deceived. The record-breaking mergers in 2015 may not have been beneficial for the involved companies, as history shows that merging two struggling companies often results in one larger failure.

If we can avoid bankrupting companies and/or companies losing most of their stock values, our portfolio would be improved substantially. Some companies make bad bets and lose, such as Enron betting on energy futures. Here are some signs of bad situations.

- Foreign companies. I do not have too much luck in developing countries, especially their stocks of small companies. They include China, Ireland and Israel to name a few. However, as of 2019, many large Chinese companies are doing very well.
- When the P/E is too good, find out why. If the P/E is too bad, stay away.
- P/PFC should be greater than 0 and less than 50. Even a healthy cash flow may not be able to service the debt if it is huge. Hence, compare the cash flow to Debt/Equity.
- Altman Z-Score. I prefer a score above 3, a sign not to be bankrupt. However, Z-Score is not designed for financial sectors.
- Beneish M-Score. I prefer a score less than -2.22, a sign that the earnings is not manipulated. Both Z-Score and M-Score are available from GuruFocus.com for a fee.
- Z-Score metrics are: "Working Capital / Total Assets" (A), "Retained Earnings / Total Assets" (B), "Earnings Before Interest & Taxes / Total Assets" (C), "Market Cap / Total Liabilities" (D) and "Sales / Total Assets" (E).
Z-Score = 1.2 A + 1.4 B + 3.3 C +.6 D + E
- Skip companies with bond ratings less than B.

- New government regulations such as taking out the credit for solar panels.
- Extraordinary profits such as Timber Liquidator and many banks in 2007-2008.
- Accounting manipulation: Excessive buying of stocks to boost Earnings per Share, excessive loans to officers, companies betting on futures such as Enron, too many one-time charges and reinstating the previous earnings.
- Skip thinly-traded stocks especially those stocks with the majority owned by a few owners.

The current financial statements could be the best source to look for them. If you read something you do not understand, be cautious.

We need to consistently monitor our stock holdings and sell them before they lose most of their value. I Recommend use stops.

This is why we need to have a focused investment portfolio of about 10 stocks; the number depends on your time available for investing. To illustrate, I have about 10 stocks with larger investments and about 100 stocks in smaller purchases. I would likely spend more time in monitoring the 10 stocks than the rest.

#Filler: Why do poor countries remain poor?

One reason is suffering from repeated natural disasters such as earthquakes and hurricanes.

Even though the U.S. has been spending a lot of resources on Puerto Rico, some politicians want to be kings and queens as they do not care about their citizens.

#Filler: One way to evaluate a company

https://www.youtube.com/watch?v=fGVtypWv04Y

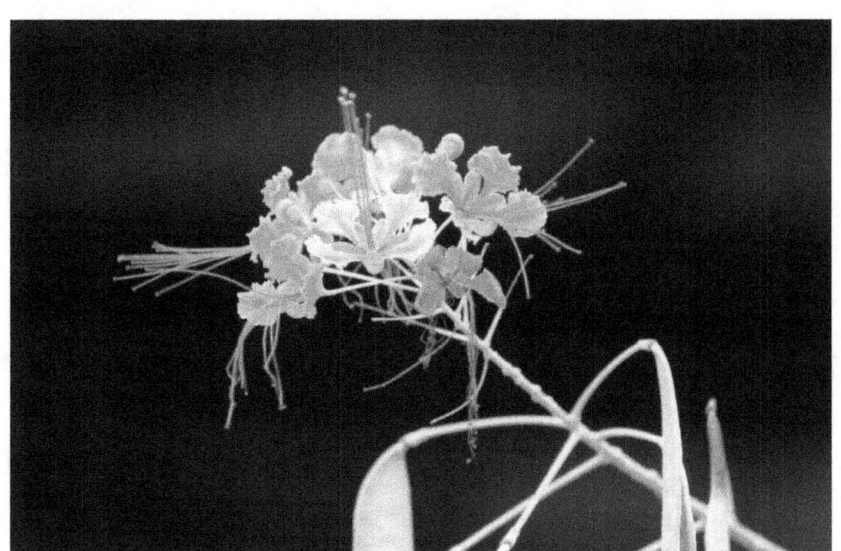

9 Avoid bankrupting companies

Avoid the bankrupting companies at all costs. Here are some hints that a company is going bankrupt:

- I had several companies that had lost most of their stock values. It turns out that most were Chinese companies. I did have some losers from Mexico, Israel and Ireland. I believe most were set up to cheat investors. Most if not all had 'rosy' financial statements. Avoid them, especially small companies in emerging countries.
- Many U.S. companies failed due to fraud, poor management, and/or the management betting wrongly. When the CEO is using the company as his own AMT, or having an extravagant lifestyle, watch out. If they promise you a return doubling the current rate of return of the market, listen to your wise mother: there is no free lunch. Despite so many real examples, still fools are born every day, because greed is a human nature.
- Do not follow the 'commentators' on TV. They have their own hidden agenda which usually is not in your interest.
- Many companies fail due to their lack of ability to pay back their loans. Except for specific industries and situations, avoid companies with high debt (Debt/Equity over 50%). Financial institutions and companies that have high debt in order to finance their products for their customers such as utilities are the exceptions.
- I have a screen named Big Losers beating the market by more than 600% in Early Recovery (a phase defined by me). However, some bankrupt companies are not included in the database which is termed as survivor bias. Hence, the actual result is far worse than the 600%. I still use this screen but skip these companies using the following yardsticks.
    - The companies are usually safe with high Free Cash Flow / Equity and high Expected Profit / Stock Price.
    - The following are red flags: low Free Cash Flow / Equity, high Inventory and high Receivable (esp. relative to its Payable), high P/B (over 30) and high net Debt/Equity (over 1 to 3 depending on the industry).
    - P/PFC should be greater than 0 and less than 50. A healthy cash flow may not be able to service the debt if it is too huge. Hence, compare it to Debt/Equity. Compare the cash flow per year to debt obligations per year.

- New government regulations could bankrupt an industry. What would happen when the U.S. takes out the rebates and subsidies of solar panels? When the U.S. banned solar panels from China, one of my Chinese stocks went bankrupt. Also, the government bailed out bankrupt companies such as Chrysler (that I made a good profit from) and AIG Fannie Mae in 2008.
- Serious lawsuits- Most U.S. companies are required to file this information in their financial reports.
- Obsolete products. Newspapers, retail and similar products would be replaced by the internet. The opposite is new products such as virtual reality products.
- Many companies run out of money during the development phase of the major products. Many are too optimistic in their business plans.
- If you expect the market will recover in 2 years, ensure the company's cash and net income can support their burn rate for at least two more years.
- Many investing sites (most require subscriptions) have safety scores.
- If the Beneish M-Score is greater than -2.22, the company is likely an accounting manipulator.
- Choose companies with Z-Score higher than 3; it is not applicable to financial companies. Both M-Score and Z-Score are available from GuruFocus, a paid subscription. Z-Score does not work for financial institutions.
- Z-Score metrics are: "Working Capital / Total Assets" (A), "Retained Earnings / Total Assets" (B), "Earnings Before Interest & Taxes / Total Assets" (C), "Market Cap / Total Liabilities" (D) and "Sales / Total Assets" (E).
Z-Score = 1.2 A + 1.4 B + 3.3 C +.6 D + E
- Market timing- It does not always work, but it is far better to follow a proven technique than not. It is far safer to take money out of the market when the market is too risky or is plunging. The big losers are companies that provide non-essential products in a downturn.
- Small companies could be risky but very profitable. Typically, they have a low stock price (less than $5), small market cap (less than 50 M), low sales (less than $25 M) and low institutional ownership (less than 5%).
- Avoid companies when their own bond ratings are not equal to AAA or AA (www.moodys.com).

- The fall of a sector such as oil in 2015 could drive the related companies, or even a country to the brink of bankruptcy.

Investing is risky to start with. However, investing especially in stocks has been proven to be the best vehicle to beat inflation.

An example from a guru on Micron

On 5/22/2023, I have been looking for info on shorting MU (Micron). There was a YouTube article on MU with a good decent way to evaluate this stock and is quite appropriate for most other stocks too.

The web site: https://www.youtube.com/watch?v=X1W_qVal1ik

I agree you should read the Form 10-K for the potential stocks to trade. It is quite hard to get the data for the last 9 years, and data for the last five years are appropriate for me. His basic metrics are:

Metric	9-Yr Avg,	Current Yr[1]	Finviz
Revenue Growth	8%	-53%	Sales Q/Q
Earnings (EBITDA) Growth	15%	-206%	EPS Q/Q
Strong Free Cash	13%	N/A	P/FCF
Debt / EBITDA <3X	1.0X	0.26	Debt / EQ
Well Priced (EV/EBITDA)[2]	5.7X	7.11	
		49	P/E
		110	Forward P/E

[1] Most are from Finviz and EV/EBITDA is from Yahoo!Finance.
[2] It is similar to P/E except considering many metrics such as taxes. The only consideration is MU's second (could be the first depending on how you link Hong Kong and other Asian countries) is China. China is developing their own memory chips. The politics between the US and China should also be considered, especially when China is the primary customer for most U.S. chip companies.

From the P/E, Forward P/E and Sales Q/Q and EPS Q/Q, I would consider more to short this short than buying it.

Links
After I wrote this article, China bans Micron due to "national security", which is the same argument for banning Huawei. Micron: https://www.youtube.com/watch?v=dy9vhwXN1SY

#Filler: G7
G7 in 2023 without China does not make any sense., so is 'de-risk'. These nations finally realized they could not decouple with China without hurting themselves. China is #1 in GDP (adjusted to purchase power) and #1 in global trade.

We are repeating history: bad mouthing China for not opening ports for trades, importing opium as a nation, using force to semi colonize China and stealing all the silver.

Section III: Selling stocks

We sell stocks when the reasons to own no longer apply by a good margin. In most cases, the sell decision should be based on data more than one quarter.

I sold ALU when it gained 40% in a few weeks' time. It gained more than 300% later when it was acquired. For rising stocks, we should adjust the stop orders. Do a mental stop order instead of just a stop order to avoid flash crashes. When the price of a stock purchased below a specified order, you place a market order to sell it. Use trailing stops for appreciated stocks.

10   When to sell a stock

We sell stocks when the reasons for owning them no longer apply by a significant margin. In most cases, the decision to sell should be based on data spanning more than one quarter.

For example, I sold ALU after it gained 40% in a few weeks, only to see it rise over 300% later when it was acquired. For rising stocks, it's wise to adjust stop orders. Consider using mental stop orders instead of formal stop orders to avoid being caught in flash crashes. A mental stop order involves setting a price threshold in your mind and selling the stock if it falls below that level. For appreciated stocks, trailing stops can be effective.

Reasons to Sell a Stock
There are numerous reasons to sell a stock, which can be categorized as follows:

Personal Reasons
1. **Meeting Targets/Objectives**:
    Sell when your investment goals are met. This could be a 10% gain in a short-term swing trade, a specific return (e.g., x%) within 4 months for a short-term trade, or a y% gain after a year for long-term investments. Define x and y based on your risk tolerance and trading frequency.

    For example, during the August 2015 market correction, I bought four stocks in one day and placed sell orders at 10% above my purchase price. I sold one stock within a day and another within a month. This strategy works sometimes, but not always.

Stay disciplined and avoid second-guessing your decisions. If the market is volatile, consider using a higher percentage threshold for your sell orders.

2. **Realizing a Mistake**:
   Acknowledge when you've made a mistake, whether due to poor analysis, bad data, unexpected fraud, lawsuits, or unforeseeable events. It's better to exit with a small loss than to hold on and risk a larger one. I use a 25% loss threshold for long-term strategies and a 10% (or less) threshold for short-term strategies.

   Determine whether the loss is due to a mistake or simply bad luck. If it's a mistake, learn from it. Diversification helps ensure that one bad loss doesn't significantly impact your portfolio. Stop-loss orders are useful, except during flash crashes.

3. **Overexposure to a Sector**:
   If you hold too many stocks in the same sector, consider selling some to improve diversification. However, if the sector is performing well, you may want to overweight it temporarily at the expense of diversification. Set limits on how many sectors you hold.

4. **Need for Cash**:
   Sell stocks if you need cash for living expenses or other financial obligations.

5. **Tax Considerations**:
   Selling losers can help reduce your tax burden, but tax considerations should not be the primary reason for selling. Take advantage of favorable tax treatment for long-term capital gains. Sell losers within the short-term limit (currently one year) and sell winners after 365 days. Check current tax laws for specifics.

   You can also harvest tax losses by selling losers and buying back similar stocks (or the same stock after 31 days to avoid wash sale rules).

6. **Lower Tax Opportunities**:
   In some cases, you can pay minimal federal income taxes on long-term capital gains if your income falls below a specific tax bracket (15% as of 2015). Check current tax laws and evaluate whether selling winners for a potential buyback makes sense.

Market Timing
7. **Market or Sector Plunge**:
   Sell stocks or reduce exposure to a sector if the market or sector experiences a significant downturn. During temporary peaks, evaluate which stocks to sell based on fundamentals to raise cash for future buying opportunities.

Deteriorating Fundamentals
8. **Better Opportunities**:
   If other stocks offer better appreciation potential, consider replacing underperforming stocks in your portfolio. While this may incur brokerage fees and taxes, it can improve the overall quality and growth potential of your portfolio.

9. **Declining Fundamentals**:
   Sell a stock if the company's fundamentals deteriorate. Compare the current fundamentals (e.g., P/E ratio, earnings growth, debt/equity ratio) to those at the time of purchase. For example, Apple's fundamentals declined between 2013 and 2015, making it a good candidate for selling.

   If a stock has peaked and started to decline, or is heading toward bankruptcy, sell it quickly.

Warning Signs of Deteriorating Fundamentals
Evaluate your stocks at least every six months and monitor daily news using tools like Seeking Alpha's portfolio function. Key warning signs include:

- **Decreasing Cash Flow**: While not a strong predictor of appreciation, declining cash flow can indicate survival risks. Cash flow is hard to manipulate.
- **Lawsuits**: Assess the seriousness of any new or pending lawsuits. Minor lawsuits can often be ignored.
- **Sales Drop**: A significant drop in sales is a red flag, though seasonal fluctuations should be considered.

- **Management Issues**: Deteriorating return on equity (ROE) or extravagant CEO behavior (e.g., excessive loans to executives) can signal trouble.
- **Operational Problems**: Product recalls, stolen trade secrets, or data breaches (e.g., Boeing's 737 MAX issues) are serious concerns.
- **Competitive Threats**: A successful competitor product or loss of market share can harm a company's prospects.
- **Insider Selling**: Heavy insider selling, especially by multiple executives, is a warning sign.
- **Regulatory Scrutiny**: Attention from the SEC or other government agencies usually indicates problems.
- **Accounting Red Flags**: Deceptive practices, increasing receivables or inventory, frequent earnings restatements, or invalid "one-time charges" are concerning.
- **Market Plunge**: A broad market downturn can signal trouble for individual stocks.

Hints that the fundamentals are degrading

Evaluate the stocks you own at least every 6 months and check their daily news at least once a week that can be easily done using Seeking Alpha's portfolio function.

- The cash flow is decreasing fast. Cash flow is not a particularly good predictive indicator for appreciation, but a good indicator on whether the company will survive. This metric is very hard to manipulate.
- A new or pending lawsuit. Check out how serious the lawsuit is and be aware that a minor lawsuit can be ignored. Companies always sue against each other.
- A big drop in sales. Do not be alarmed when a new product, or a new drug is going to replace a major product. Compare sales to the same quarter of prior year to avoid seasonal fluctuations (Q-to-Q info I available from Finviz.com).
- Management deteriorates- One hint is the deteriorating ROE from the last quarter.
- The extravagant lifestyle of the CEO and the many easy loans to officers.
- Poor operations. They include recalls of products such as the GM recall on ignition switches, product secrets being stolen and

customers' credit card info being stolen. Boeing's 747-Max is a warning call.
- A successful product from the competitor, or the current product is losing its market share, or becoming a low-profit commodity.
- Insiders and/or institutional investors are dumping the companies' stocks far more than the averages (2% for me) especially in heavy volumes and by more than one insider. Info is available from Finviz.

    - Have more than one insider dumping a lot of the stock within a month and no insider purchase in that month. Have more than one insider decrease their holdings by more than 10%.
    - When the SEC or any government agency pays attention to a company, it usually means bad news.
    - Deceptive accounting practices have been discovered.
    - Increasing receivable and/or inventory at an alarming rate.
    - Earnings have been restated too many times.
    - Short percentage is increasing fast – someone found something wrong with the company.
    - The invalidity of 'one-time charges'.
    - Abnormal return rate of the company's pension fund comparing to the average of the companies in the same sector.
    - Too many and too costly reconstructing charges.
    - The stock price does not move up with good news. It shows the price has peaked.
    - The accumulation amount is far less than the sold amount. When the stock price is up, the accumulation is less than the sold stocks when the stock price was down the last time. It indicates that no more accumulation is ahead and hence the stock will be down most likely.

Afterthoughts

- Another article on this topic.
  http://buzz.money.cnn.com/2013/04/05/stocks-sell/
  An article from Investopedia. Nothing new but it is worth having the same second opinion.

http://www.investopedia.com/financial-edge/0412/5-tips-on-when-to-sell-your-stock.aspx

- It also depends on your strategies. I sell most of my stocks in my momentum portfolio within a month. At least one strategy I know of does not keep any stock during the peak stage of the market cycle – the easiest time to make money but also the riskiest time.

   If you use charts for trading, sell the stocks that are below your moving averages or other technical analysis indicators. Personally, I do not use charts for making sell decisions due to my limited time.
- Sell when the company is heading into bankruptcy as described before. The red flags are: 1. Negative cash flow. 2. Heavy insiders dumping the stocks. 3. Pending major lawsuit. 4. Fraud from the management.
- Risky periods for a stock.
   Earnings announcement (4 times a year), settling a major lawsuit and/or during an FDA event in approving a drug are risky periods for a stock. A fluctuation more than 5% in either direction is normal. Some use options to buy insurance. Most ignore it. For the majority of the time, heavy insider purchase is a good indicator. There are rumors (or educated guesses) on earnings before their announcements. Zacks is supposed to be a good subscription for earnings estimates.

Selling a winner

Let your profits rise while protecting them. For example, Tesla quadrupled in value in six months, and similar gains have been seen with Amazon and Yelp. If you're unsure what to do, consider these strategies:

- Sell half of your position.
- Sell an amount equal to your initial investment.
- Use trailing stops to lock in gains. I did not do this when my GameStop stock appreciated by 300% and it turned out for far more appreciation. Guilty as charged.

You do not want to sell these rocket stocks even if their fundamentals do not make sense. Buffett does not touch these rocket stocks and he usually misses these big gains. However, many of these rocket stocks such as BRRY (Blackberry) will eventually fall losing most of their value. I bet the institutional investors move the market in either direction and usually they read the same analysts' reports. You profit as a contrarian if you have a good reason to act against the herd.

The following example uses a 10% trailing stop – mine is a little different from the official trailing stop described in the link section. Set the stop at 10% of the current price (i.e., 10% less than the current price), not the purchase price. You need to change the stop when the price rises but do not change it when the price falls. Review your stops every month or more frequently if time allows.

To illustrate, when the stock price rises to 100, set the stop at 90. When the stock price falls to 90, sell the stock at the market price. When the stock price rises to 200, change the stop price at 180.

The stop should also be set according to how volatile the stock is. Some stocks are more volatile than others. Most charts show the resistance line. This line assumes the stock price should not fall below this line in normal fluctuations. Set the stop at 2% below this line so your stock will not be stopped out in theory.

Do not stop orders on stocks with low volumes as they can be manipulated, especially after hours. In this case, you just place market orders to sell them.

To avoid flash crashes, do not place stop orders. Instead, do it mentally (mental stop is my term). When you see that the stock falls below your stop with no sign of a flash crash, sell the stock using a market order.

Of course, there is no bullet-proof scheme. This one should work in the long run. This is my suggestion only, so examine whether it works for you. Small cap and/or stocks with small average volumes fluctuate more.

Examples
I have too many bad examples of selling the stocks too early and sometimes holding them too long.

I made over 40% in a few weeks on ALU, but it went up more than 300% in the next two years. It was acquired in early 2016 by Nokia paying a good premium. I was right that ALU had a lot of valuable patents and I was wrong to dump it when I found out Cisco did not have any intention to acquire it – a big mistake by Cisco and the U.S.

FOSL is another example to teach us to use mental stop loss. FOSL was priced at $33.70 on 1/4/2010. Its fundamentals were just fine with an expected E/P (expected earnings yield) at 6% but decreasing earnings. It gained 115% later in 2010 - not expected.

On 1/3/2011, the expected E/P was still at around 6% and improving earnings. It gained 9% for the year – a little disappointing.

On 1/3/2012, the expected E/P was 7% and a huge earnings growth. Now, we expected a better performance for the year and it did by gaining 20%.

On 1/3/2013, the expected E/P was about 6% and the earnings gain was respectable. It gained 28% to $121. So far, so good.

On 1/2/2014, the E/P and the earnings growth were about the same as in 1/3/2013. However, it lost 7% for the year while SPY (an ETF simulating the market) gained 12%. There was no warning. Did the institutional investors lose the interest of this stock?

On 1/2/2015, the E/P was 7% and the earnings growth was about the same as the previous year. It lost 69% (vs. SPY's 0% return with dividends)!

From 1/4/2010 to 1/3/2016, the annualized return of FOSL is 0% (vs. SPY's 13%). Actually, after dividends, SPY should have an annualized return of about 15%. The lessons gained here are:

- Fundamentals (using EP and earnings growth in this example) may not always work. Otherwise, 2015 should have the same gain as 2014.
- The rosy outlook of the stock may be priced in already. When the outlook fails to materialize, the stock tanks.

Links: Fidelity Video: Trailing Stop Loss. 2 3
https://www.fidelity.com/learning-center/trading/trailing-stops-video
https://www.youtube.com/watch?v=l7EHWyOrfu4

https://www.investopedia.com/terms/t/trailingstop.asp

11 Examples of overpriced stocks

In 2011, Netflix, LinkedIn, and Facebook were widely considered overvalued. Here's how to assess whether a stock is overpriced:

- **Reward/Risk Ratio**: If a stock has a 30% chance of rising and a 50% chance of falling, it's overvalued by 20%.
- **P/E Ratio**: Compare the current P/E to its five-year average. For example, if Netflix's P/E was 60 compared to a five-year average of 30, it was overvalued by 100%.
- **Momentum Plays**: Buying high and selling higher can work with stop-loss orders, but I prefer buying low and selling high.

More notes:
- The 'E' in P/E can be either expected (same as forward) earnings or based on the last 12 months (same as trailing or historical). It has been proven that the 'expected' is a better indicator than the 'historical'. AAII demonstrated this by comparing the performances of the expected PEG screen and the historical PEG screens over a long period of time.
- Fools who invested in the high P/E stocks and did not do their due diligence in 2000 had parted with their money fast. I could not convince my friends to take money off their internet stocks. It is similar to asking the lottery winners not to buy lottery tickets.
- Buying an expensive stock is like over paying for a hot dog cart in NYC for $100,000. The buyer will sell many hot dogs, but the rate of return of the investment will be minimal, and it will never recover the initial investment. "Buy high and sell higher" is a momentum play. It works if it is played with stops, but I prefer to "Buy low and sell high".
- Following a decent and proven investing strategy consistently should lead to success through persistence and adjustments. In the long term, a bad strategy always loses money.
- When the market favors growth / momentum (vs. value), it is OK to buy stocks with prices higher than the intrinsic values by a small percentage. The tide is on your side. However, be attentive to any indication that the market is changing direction.
- NFLX has an average annual return rate of 177% vs. SPY's 14% from 1/3/2011 to 1/3/2020 without considering dividends. Hence, a trailing stop would do the job for the rocket stock.

12   Should you hold stocks forever?

There are many examples that you should hold onto some stocks forever such as Apple, Netflix, Amazon and Google. Interestingly there are more opposite examples such as AIG and Lehman Brothers. Hence, there is no right or wrong answer. Always continually monitor your stock holdings and the sectors they are in.

Even IBM could suffer its dips when it does not react to its market and / or make the wrong strategic decision. The Washington Post has to react to the free articles from the internet.

I have set up guidelines on when to sell. One selling indicator is when those shares lose over 25%. We have to admit that we have made a mistake, or the fundamentals of the stock have changed. Evaluate the fundamentals of the purchased stocks periodically.

Boston Chicken is one of my many big losers. I could use the money I lost to have chicken dinner every night for the rest of my life! This kind of thinking is not healthy. I decided not to buy any restaurant stock again and that is not rational either. It is an art to sell a loser, or wait for its potential recovery. From my experiences, it is better to sell the loser.

If you have a historical database, you can test out your strategy on when to sell and adjust the sell criteria accordingly. Do not try to fit data to your strategy.

Never fall in love with a stock and never be afraid to buy back a sold stock. Use fundamental metrics for making a buy/sell decision.

Taxes and diversification

Tax should not be a major consideration in selling a stock. However, you may postpone selling losers in December if your tax rate (so your tax loss value) will be better next year. If you need to offset short-term capital gains, sell some losers eligible for short-term capital losses. Postpone selling a winner to a month or so, if it can be eligible for long-term capital gain.

When your stock appreciates many, many times and you're close to your life expectancy age, hold it and the cost basis will step up to the day you pass away. Instruct your heirs to buy a newspaper to get the prices of your stocks you hold or instruct your heirs to inform your broker on the unavoidable day. Today's tax law provides a range of days around the date of death; check the current tax laws.

Instead of selling a stock with huge gain, consider options: 1. give it to your children who have lower tax brackets, 2. give it to charity, and 3. save it for your estate.

When the market is plunging as detected by market timing techniques, sell most of your holdings. Be warned that market timing does not always work.

No stock is sacred

That's why we need to churn the portfolio by replacing the bad stocks with better ones. More examples of failing companies that had been very promising at one time:

- The bankrupt companies due to competition: Circuit City (due to BestBuy) and BlockBuster (due to Netflix).
- The failing internet companies in 2000 and the financial institutions in 2008.
- HP when PCs, servers and printers are no longer kings.
- BestBuy killed Circuit City and then it is being eaten alive by Amazon, Walmart, Costco and BJ. However, it recovered in 2014.
- Many retailers went bankrupt. I lost count of so many of the retailers in the Boston area alone.

Filler: Dream high

I heard this. The girl wanted to be a president when she grew up. She went to a circus and she said she wanted to be a clown. Her wise father said, "You can be a president and a clown at the same time". Reality?

Should we modify the Constitution to ban our presidents from tweeting especially in private places?

It is a laughing stock for injecting disinfectants to cure the virus. At least we fix the racial discrimination when everyone has been bleached.

I am neutral in politics. I complained a lot about Obama.

13   Monitor your traded stocks

After buying or shorting a stock, actively monitor its performance and any new developments. Here's how:

1. **Use Stop Orders**: Protect your portfolio with stop or trailing stop orders, especially for rising stocks.
2. **Stay Informed**: Read articles about your stocks using platforms like Finviz, Seeking Alpha, or MarketWatch.
3. **Organize Watchlists**: Create multiple watchlists for different strategies (e.g., long-term value stocks vs. short-term momentum stocks).
4. **Track Performance**: Monitor your stocks' performance and sector diversification to avoid overexposure.

More notes:

- Categorize the stocks by sectors, and check the performances of these sectors.
- Keep track of the holding days for better tax treatments of long-term capital gains in taxable accounts. You may sell short=term losers in taxable accounts.
- To generate income, use covered calls.
- Market timing and sector timing.

Final Thoughts

Investing is both an art and a science. While no strategy is foolproof, staying disciplined, informed, and adaptable can help you navigate the market's ups and downs. Regularly review your portfolio, learn from your mistakes, and don't fall in love with any stock.

Section IV: Other sources

Investing, like health, requires discipline, research, and action. Use tools like Seeking Alpha and Fidelity to stay informed, but always be cautious of market noise and overhyped strategies. Diversify your portfolio, monitor market conditions, and apply what you learn to make better investment decisions.

14   Lessons from a popular book?

I recently read a popular book on how to make money in the stock market. While the strategies worked for the author, they may not work for you. Here's why:

- **Overuse of Strategies**: The book has been read by tens of thousands of people. When a strategy becomes widely adopted, it often loses its effectiveness. If you follow the same approach, you'll likely end up with the same stocks as everyone else, reducing your chances of outperforming the market.
- **Buffett's Philosophy**: The book is based on Warren Buffett's investment philosophy. While some of Buffett's strategies work, others don't, and some opportunities are inaccessible to retail investors. Given Buffett's mediocre returns in recent years, blindly following his approach might not be the best use of your time and money.
- **Lack of Diversification**: The book doesn't emphasize diversification, which is crucial for managing risk. Even good stocks can lose half their value unexpectedly. If you have $50,000 or less, consider holding three stocks across different sectors, with one being an ETF.
- **Ignoring Market Timing**: The book doesn't address market timing, which can be critical during market crashes. Without considering market conditions, you could lose significant value in your portfolio.
- **Value Traps**: The book suggests finding stocks at a 50% discount, but such opportunities are rare in a bullish market. When you do find them, be cautious—there's usually a reason for the steep discount. These opportunities are more common during market recoveries.
- **Margin of Safety**: The concept of a "margin of safety" is often highlighted, but my limited testing shows it's not a reliable predictor of stock performance.

- **Reading Annual Reports**: The book emphasizes reading annual reports, which can be useful. Here's a helpful video on how to do it: How to Read Annual Reports.

15 Using Seeking Alpha effectivley

Seeking Alpha is a valuable resource for investors. Here's how to make the most of it:

- **Portfolio Function**: Use the portfolio feature to track stocks you own or are interested in. You'll receive alerts for news and articles related to those stocks. This function is similar to Finviz and some broker platforms, though smaller stocks may not be covered.

- **Quality Articles**: The site offers many insightful articles. Focus on those written by authors you follow, especially if their strategies align with yours (e.g., dividend investing).

- **Market Insights**: The "Market Performance via ETFs" section shows trending sectors, while "Wall Street Breakfast" provides a daily summary of market events. These tools are useful for sector rotation and identifying momentum stocks.

- **Watch Out for Pitfalls**:
  - **Promotions**: Seeking Alpha is a business, so some content is promotional. Be discerning about what applies to you.
  - **Pump and Dump Schemes**: Be cautious with reviews of small or low-volume stocks. For example, one short-seller made negative comments about EBIX, a stock I owned, but it gained 150% in a year.

Filler

Here is a good article: 60 Value Resources.

http://seekingalpha.com/article/3485446-60-best-value-investing-resources-youd-be-crazy-to-miss

16 Making sense of health and investing

I read Dr. Campbell's *The* China Study, which advocates a whole-food, plant-based diet to prevent diseases like heart disease and cancer. While this may seem unrelated to investing, there are striking parallels between the two disciplines:

- **Statistics**: Just as a plant-based diet leads to better health outcomes over time, a well-tested investment strategy with more winners than losers will outperform the market in the long run. Statistics don't lie.
- **Market Noise**: The health industry is influenced by big corporations like meat producers and fast-food chains, much like how stock promotions and TV business programs are driven by advertisers. Always do your own research.
- **Action Matters**: Many people read books but fail to apply the lessons. I recommend paper trading to practice what you learn from investment books.

Dr. Campbell's book can make you healthier, and my insights aim to make you a better investor.

17 Leveraging Fidelity's Research Tools

Fidelity offers extensive research tools for free, even without an account balance. Here's how to use them effectively:

- **Equity Summary Score**: This score has proven useful. I prefer buying stocks with a score of 8 or higher for long-term holds and shorting those with a score of 4 or lower. However, use caution—scores can sometimes be misleading. For example, in June 2020, ZM and SHOP had high scores despite poor long-term metrics.
- **P/E Ratios**:
    - **5-Year Average**: Compare a stock's current P/E to its 5-year average to identify bargains. Be cautious if the P/E is zero or negative. I prefer using forward P/E (estimated earnings).
    - **Industry Average**: Compare a company's P/E to its industry average for better context.
- **Environmental, Social & Governance (ESG)**: Useful for socially conscious investors.
- **Research Reports**: Access reports under the "Analyst Opinions and Reports" tab. Focus on those with high StarMine Relative Accuracy. Experienced investors should also review Form 10-Q and balance sheets.

- **Momentum Analysis**: Available under the "Technical Sentiment" tab, this tool compares short-term, mid-term, and long-term momentum to indicators like SMA-20, SMA-50, SMA-200, and RSI(14).
- **Top-Down Approach**: When the market is up, select the best stocks in the best sectors or industries using the "Comparisons" tab.

An example

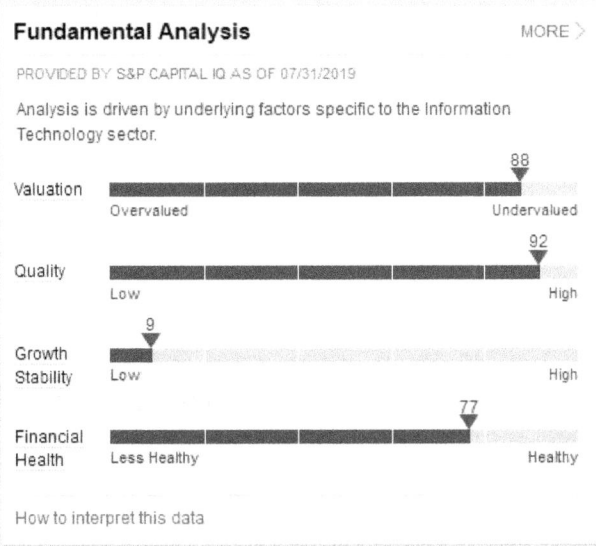

Most stock research sites group the related metrics, weigh them and have a score. The following is my guess only and over-simplified. Basically, they should have 3 scores: Valuation (for long-term trades), Momentum (for short-term trades) and Combined (Valuation + Momentum). Safety or Financial Health is whether the stock is safe (i.e., the chance to go bankrupt).

Valuation. Forward P/E. Insider Transactions.
Quality. ROI, P/E and Debt/Equity.
Growth Stability. Q-Q Earnings.
Financial Health. Debt/Equity. Earnings.

Links
Platform tutorial: https://www.youtube.com/watch?v=fxE5577LaxE
Fidelity index funds: https://www.youtube.com/watch?v=xdEunmLrhb4
Investing tips: https://www.youtube.com/watch?v=twMNKMhL_KY

Bonus: Experiences

It has three sections: Performances from my book series "Best Stocks", my own experiences and the experiences from gurus with my own comments.

It has been hard to keep up all my trades and publish them in a book. Section #1 solves this problem as they are based on real recommendations.

Section #2 are what I read from articles and YouTube videos from Gurus. If they are in English, most likely a link is included. I add my own comments.

Do not act without consulting to your financial advisor first. The info could be obsolete by the time you read this book. I suggest the strategies and how we approach on certain sectors and situations, and hopefully they would work. The market is not always rational, and hence first test out the strategy described and use stops to protect your portfolio.

Section 1: Performance form "Best Stocks" series

1   Past Performances

Management Summary as of 7/01/21
The books in this series should be available on 7/15 and 12/15 in each year, but it is not a promise. I use the opening prices of 7/1/21 to update the performance info, so I can have more time to research stocks for this new book. Most are value stocks in the primary lists. The momentum stocks such as FAANG were doing very well in 2020, and SPY has more weights on these stocks; hence beating SPY is not easy in 2020.

This article "Past Performances" (not the rest of the book) can be freely distributed with mentioning the title of this book. This is for reference only, and I am not liable for any errors. The following performances are from my last three books in this series.

Book	Stocks	Return	Ann.	Beat SPY by[1]
Best Stocks for 2021 2nd Edition	10	20%	52%[3]	110%
Best Stocks for 2021	4	29%	52%	71%
Best Stocks to Buy from Aug, 2020	14	42%	45%	25%
Avg.		9	31%	50%	69%[2]

[1] See Methodology. "Beat SPY by" does not include commissions and dividends that would increase this ratio for winners.
[2] If you buy all stocks recommended in the primary lists (secondary lists are also described separately), you should have an annualized returns of 50% and beat SPY (representing the market) by about 69% without considering dividends and fees. If this average is less than 2%, do not buy the book until it will work again; I need to change my strategies to meet the current market conditions.
[3] CTB selected in "Best Stocks for 2021 2nd Edition" has been delisted (most likely has been acquired). It is my better winner (it returned 44% and 217% annualized on 4/22/2021), and hence the return of the portfolio should be better than the stated.

You buy this book or similar books because you expect the selected stocks are profitable. A 1,000+ page book with a poor performance record would cost you money. Even a one-page book will make you money if the recommended stocks perform, as you are paying for the exhaustive research behind the selection.

No one can predict the future performance of his or her selected stocks. Based on the last year of the books in this series, the chance of success of my selection is good for this book. If it continues to work, the price of the book is peanuts. If it does not, it would be harmful even if it is free.

I have many strategies (same as screens) and I usually choose those strategies that work well recently. The screened stocks will be compared to my own criteria with some exceptions. Hence, most are value stocks that should be better positioned to a down market. I do attempt to time the market as described in this book. I bought many of the stocks I recommended. Some buy orders have not been executed as they had risen too fast at the gate.

There are many vendors recommending stocks and showing their 'fantastic' results that they selected their favorable periods, or trading with the best prices of the day. Some showed you the returns of the big winners, but not the big losers. I will show you the performances of my last 3 books. Past performances have nothing to do with future performances. Refer to Disclaimer under Introduction.

The rest of the article describes the performances of the stocks in more detail on the last three books in this series. Each book has a primary list and any sub lists.

Book #1: "Best Stocks for 2021 2nd Edition"
Start date: 02/08/2021. End date: 07/01/2021.
CTB has been delisted as of 7/1/2021. The price on the recommended date is $35 and the price on 6/17/2021 is 40.12, and it is my best winner in this group. From my last update on 4/24/2021, it returned 44% and 217% annualized.

Symbol	Return	Annualized
BG	5%	14%
CBNK	40%	103%
CTB	N/A	N/A
CUBI	49%	126%
HMST	-1%	-1%
JEF	28%	72%
MLI	14%	36%
OPY	34%	88%
TPVG	6%	15%
UVSP	5%	13%

Average	20%	52%
SPY	10%	25%
Beat SPY by	110%	

Short-term lists

There are two bonus lists: Momentum and Short. These lists are short-term, and hence I use one month as the end dates.

Start date: 02/08/2021. End date: 03/10/2021.

Momentum (7 stocks)

Symbol	Return	Ann.
ATGE	-6%	-68%
ATRS	-11%	-134%
CMRE	15%	182%
REGI	-26%	-318%
RIO	0%	-1%
SPWH	0%	-1%
WIRE	8%	96%
Average	-3%	-35%
SPY	0%	-3%
Beat SPY by	-1100%	

Short selling betting the stocks to go down (3 stocks).

Symbol	Return	Ann.
HYLN	16%	191%
NEXT	2%	332%
RMO	40%	482%
Average	28%	335%
SPY	0%	-3%
Beat SPY by	11,571%	

Since SPY's return is close to zero, the "Best SPY by" has no meaning. This momentum list does not perform, but the short list does.

The short-term lists may not be provided in future books, as they are too volatile and have little value to readers due to time span from the initial publish date.

Book #2: "Best Stocks for 2021"

Start Date: 12/10/2020. End Date: 07/01/2021.

Besides the primary list of recommended stocks, I have several other lists. Year-End lists are short-term, and the End Date is 01/10/2021. I provide 2nd month and 3rd month holding to determine what is a better holding period for the current selection.

Summary:

List (# of stocks)	Return	Annualized	Beat SPY
Primary list (4)	29%	52%	71%
Primary list without GLD (3)	39%	71%	135%
Secondary list (6)	46%	84%	177%
Year-End list (5)	5%		68%
Secondary list for Year-End (5)	-1%		-125%
Secondary list without foreign countries (2)	14%		342%[1]

Details

1. Primary list.

Primary List (stocks = 4)	Return	Annualized	Beat SPY
DSK	84%	151%	
ESGR	20%	35%	
GLD	-4%	-7%	
OTTR	15%	27%	
Average	29%	52%	71%
SPY	14%		

2. Primary list without GLD.

Primary List (stocks = 3)	Return	Annualized	Beat SPY
DSK	84%	151%	
ESGR	20%	35%	
OTTR	15%	27%	

Average	39%	71%	135%
SPY	17%		

GLD is a hedge for inflation, and it should not be included in the primary list, but I did.

3. Secondary list.

Secondary List (stocks = 5)	Return	Annualized	Beat SPY
BCC	46%	126%	
GPI	35%	95%	
HEAR	43%	118%	
HVT	53%	144%	
HZO	75%	204%	
Average	46%	84%	177%
SPY	17%	30%	

Most of the stock selected in this list have high dumping by the insiders. It seems the insiders were wrong and they are usually not wrong.

4. Year-End Loser list.
From 12/10/2020 to 1/10/2021. Include the performances keeping this portfolio for 2 and 3 months. This is the official list for year-end losers. There are other options and they will be used for future selections.

Year-End (5 stocks)	Return	Ann %	Beat SPY	Beat SPY
Hold period	1 Month	1 Month	2 Months	3 Months
BCOR	20%	224%	28%	26%
CEPU	-10%	-114%	-10%	-17%
EEX	-8%	-94%	-3%	30%
GANG	17%	191%	38%	62%
STFC	9%	105%	1%	22%
Average	5%	63%	11%	25%
SPY	3%	37%	6%	6%
Beat SPY	68%		70%	298%

The above result suggests us to hold the stocks for 3 months instead of 1. It could be due to the better performance of GANG from 17% to 62%. SPY has a lot of growth stocks and they suffer from a dip during the third month.

4A. Year-End Loser Secondary list

Year-End (5 stocks)	Return	Ann %	Beat SPY	Beat SPY
Hold period	1 Month	1 Month	2 Months	3 Months
ADES	-4%	-47%	3%	3%
BMA	-17%	-190%	-14%	-18%
DXC	14%	163%	3%	17%
PAM	-12%	-140%	-5%	-3%
PLCE	15%	166%	68%	71%
Average	-1%		12%	14%
SPY	3%		6%	6%
Beat SPY	-125%		87%	124%

The foreign stocks do not perform, but the performance has improved immensely for holding 3 months.

4B. Year-End Loser Secondary list with US companies only.

Year-End (2 stocks)	Return	Ann %	Beat SPY	Beat SPY
Hold period	1 Month	1 Month	2 Months	3 Months
DXC	14%	163%	3%	17%
PLCE	15%	166%	68%	71%
Average	14%	164%	36%	44%
SPY	3%		6%	6%
Beat SPY	342%		464%	605%

This list turns out to have the best performance of the 3 year-end lists.

Book #3: "Best Stocks to buy from August, 2020"

The performance is the returns from 07/28/2020 to 07/01/2021 (close to the next book in the series). The average of the 14 recommended stocks beats SPY (an ETF simulating S&P 500 stocks) by 29%. **The 25% is**

unbelievable as SPY has been weighed heavily with a lot of tech stocks such as Apple, Tesla and Microsoft, and they had been increased in value substantially during this period. If you believe they will continue this trend, SPY or any ETF weighed on tech stocks would be beneficial. However, I believe they are peaking and the fall seems inevitable – it is my personal opinion. All 14 selected stocks are winners. Again, dividends and fees have not been included. CMCSA and FDX are big winners profiting from the pandemic. True EY is obtained at the time of evaluation, about a year ago.

Symbol	Sector	True EY	Return 07/01/21	Ann. Return
ABBV	Drug	7%	16%	18%
ABT	Drug	3%	16%	17%
CHE	Diversified	4%	4%	5%
CMCSA	Media	11%	32%	35%
FDX	Transport	8%	79%	85%
GTS	Health	N/A	15%	16%
JNJ	Drug	6%	12%	13%
MCK	Drug	8%	24%	26%
MSFT	Software	4%	34%	37%
SCHN	Metal	10%	163%	177%
SMCI	Computer	11%	25%	27%
UFPI	Building	10%	32%	34%
UNH	Health	9%	34%	36%
ZBRA	Computer	5%	95%	103%
Avg.			42%	45%
		SPY	33%	36%
	Beat SPY			25%

At one time UFPI was a loser.

Methodology

- 'Beat SPY by "= (Return – SPY's return) / (SPY's return) with adjustments to negative numbers.

- Dividends and fees are not included. Hence, the ratio usually looks better than it actually is.

- Past performances have nothing to do with future performances. So far, the last two books have performed well with the market conditions.

The performances are for reference only. These incredible performances are not sustainable. **Consult your financial advisor** before taking any action. The author and the publisher are not liable for any errors.

- Start date usually is the publish date, and end date usually is the publish date of the next book in the series. May add the performance for one year. Dates could be one or two days off due to non-trading days.

- Short-term trades such as Year-End strategy is usually one month duration. May add 2-month and 3-month durations for comparison.
- True EY is the earnings yield considering debts and cash. Compare it to one-year Treasuries and CDs which are basically risk free. It is the reciprocal of "EV/EBITDA". It is obtained from Yahoo!Finance (under Statistics).

- Most figures are rounded up for easy reading, but not in the calculation in "Beat SPY by".

- Once in a while, the performance is not correct due to many uncontrolled events such as delisting a stock (due to bankruptcy, merger…).

- There are older books. However, I cannot get the performances due to the survival bias (i.e. the delisted stocks are no longer in the database).

Section 2: Gurus' experiences

It has three sections: Performances from my book series "Best Stocks", my own and the guru's.

1   Pointers from short-term gurus

- Develop a trading system that fits your personality, your skill and your timing available for trading. A beginner's trading system is different from a skilled trader's system.
- Start with two or three technical indicators (SMA is my favorite), current events more than fundamentals. Study daily news about the stock you want to trade.
- Even with a win-loss ratio of 50%, you still can make a lot of money by protecting your portfolio with stop loss and your profits with trailing stops. Define and enforce your exit strategy.
- Knowledge is everything, and hence learn from the best traders. There are schools (some on-line) teaching folks how to trade. It is less expensive than paying your tuition via actual trading. This book and most other books are a good start and most cost effective. Many old books (so is this book 15 years later if I do not update it) and old techniques may not work today; today we have no commission brokers, and most technical indicators are available free.

- Beginners cannot beat professionals without luck. You do not gain knowledge by paper trading. Start small. Never risk the money you cannot afford to lose.
- Need basic capital for trading and a laptop to start. Plus living expenses for a few months if you trade full time. Prepare your new venture psychologically. Be emotionally detached in investing. Silence is golden, the rule I just violated. Your friends will not share their wins but blame, and it affects your ego and your trading.
I know many made so much in 2000 and in early 2021 that they quitted their day jobs, and then they found out they had big losses later.

- Diversify but not overdiversify. Most of us can handle about three trades simultaneously, or more if your holding period is longer than a day.
- When the number of new heights exceeds the new lows by a large margin (determined by you as all markets are different), consider sell (the market could be peaking). Buy, vice versa.
- Day traders may close their positions (more long than short) at the end of the day, especially on late Fridays to avoid unexpected events and interests. The exception is when the market is surging. Learn money

- management – never bet it all in one trade. Do not trade in the first hour of the market.
- When you have three unsuccessful trades in a row, it is time to take a break and/or switch to paper trading. Better double your bet on winning stocks, and not the other way round.
- Record all your trades and the results in a trade journal. Review it and learn from your successes and losses periodically.
- Modify your trade system according to your gained knowledge and the market trend. Test it out with no or minimum money until you are comfortable.

Links: https://www.youtube.com/watch?v=qL7Z7XQ6tPA

2   Tips from Peter Lynch

He made a lot of money for his investors in Magellan's fund. I came in late to his funds, but I also left early when he retired early in 1990. Many did not want to leave due to the potential tax burdens. His successors never achieved the same performance in Peter's 9 years with the fund. Peter was smart enough to know that his fund was so big that it was the market, and no one could beat the market by that margin consistently.

The following is my summary and my comments on his tips from several YouTube videos
https://www.youtube.com/watch?v=IhnfqbliGC4
https://www.youtube.com/watch?v=J1DFMXL2kXE
https://www.youtube.com/watch?v=0lYU40sZsUo

1. Study more stocks and pick the best.
   Same as doing your homework.
2. Emotionally detached. Do not sell at the bottom.
   No one can predict the market and is correct constantly. My article could limit the loss and save the cash for reentering the market. Buying at early recovery is very profitable.
3. Investing in companies whose products / services you understand.
   We all have expertise in our own field and the mall is a better place to find good consumer products.
   However, today's mall is pretty much destroyed by Amazon.com. In this case, you should buy Amazon.com, and short many retail outfits and the mall owners. Also check whether Amazon.com has reached its growth potential or not. You may miss Zoom, but as of 10/2020, the stock is too expensive. With the momentum, I do not want to short this stock.

Made big profits in McDonald's as the sales/profits had been rising for years. However, most of the profits were derived from real estate holdings.

I do not totally agree with it. There are many companies that we do not know but we can learn and understand what their technologies could be potentially profitable. Buffett did not invest in Apple as he did not use a mobile phone, but his research team should.

4. Easier to beat the professionals than expected.
   Fund managers have to stick with large companies and they cannot time the market. You
5. Invest in profitable small companies.
   Small companies have a lot of risk, but they also have higher profit potential than matured companies.
6. Find a few good stocks particularly at their early stage.
   It is harder to do than say. When the stock moves from Russell 2000 to Russell 1000 (promoting from an index for smaller stocks), they could be candidates. He recommends to keep 5 to 10 stocks for individuals
   A fast growing stock may never be too late to invest.
   We can find these stocks earlier than the professionals and many funds cannot invest in these stocks.
7. Buy growing companies and sell the matured companies that their markets have been saturated (i.e. no place to grow). That's why P/E may not work all the time; you need to consider quarter-to-quarter sales growth and earnings growth; actually year-to-year for the past 5 or even more years is important.
8. Buy good cynical stocks at the bottom and sell at the top.
   It is hard to determine the bottom and the top. However, you need to ensure the company would not go bankrupt by ensuring the income can service its debt.
9. Do not be afraid to buy the stocks that have doubled the prices as long as the fundamentals are still increasing such as Microsoft and Apple.
10. Consider turnaround companies.
    Check the balance sheet. They need cash for turnaround such as promoting new products/services. Skip those companies that have hints of failure of the turnaround. Disney was one at one time by using the hidden assets. Brand names are not included in the financial statements.
11. Do not sell when you double the profit or you lose 10%.
    Agree if they are good stocks. I have some 'good' stocks that went to almost zero value; one Chinese solar company was due to the U.S. policy banning it to the U.S. market.
12. Sell a stock when the fundamentals decline.
    That's where my score for fundamentals or Fidelity's Equity Summary Score comes in. If you do not have time to research

stock, buy ETFs that simulate the market. It is not Lynch's idea (as a fund manager) but mine and Buffett's.
13. Do not sell when they have short-term problems such as not meeting the earnings prediction.
14. Do not time the market. I do not agree with this as I have proven simple market timing could save you further losses when the market crashes.
15. In the long term, stocks beat bonds and CDs. Investing in retirement accounts allows our investments to grow, compounding and deferring taxes.

3   Charles Munger: 12 common mistakes

Check out the link
https://www.youtube.com/watch?v=W0W44Ykdojw

I add my experiences and also my own common mistakes from mistake #14 and on.

1. Ignore jealousy and resentment.
- I published an article titled "Amazing Returns". I received a lot of resentment and attacks. If they just bought the stocks I recommended, they should have made a lot of money.
- A reader gave me the worst rating on one of my books in the "Best Stock Series" while most ratings were the best. She complained the book was 'too thin'. Most books on investing are 250 pages (6*9), and mine is 300 pages. If she had followed the recommendations of the book, she would have beaten the market by a wide margin.
2. Never open-spend your income. I am guilty of under spending my income.
3. Grab all opportunities.
- I did not invest heavily in Chinese ETFs such as FXI during China's rise, and I did not short them when the U.S. delisted many Chinese stocks.
- I did not take the opportunities when the pandemic was confirmed, but I did invest in commodities due to inflation.
4. Keep learning. I should have read my own book again as I have committed the same investing mistakes.
5. Deserve what you want.
6. Understand your competency. If you do not have time, or desire to learn investing, buy ETFs.
7. Be a survivor. Never put all eggs in one basket (i.e. diversify).
8. Practice the right approach. Check whether your approach is appropriate to the current market conditions from my interpretation.

9. Understand your trade. If it is a value stock, emphasize fundamentals and allow more time for the market to realize its value. Have an exit plan.
10. Invest in trust. He may mean trusting the management of the company.
11. Survive competently as you can.
12. Don't pity yourself. Learn from your failure and ensure that you will not repeat the same mistake. I am guilty as charged.
13. Don't diversify. I interpret "Don't diversify excessively". I believe 5 to 10 stocks with less than 25% of the stocks in the same sector.
14. Don't be afraid of price appreciation as long as the story why you bought the stock has not changed.

4   Making 20% return year after year

This web article (https://www.youtube.com/watch?v=G9xVNjJBSzg) is interesting. Most ideas have been described in this book. I include their pointers here with my own comments:

1. Invest, not speculate. Treat your stock as a company (Buffett's idea). Buy low and sell high. No need to watch your stock every day. Review it periodically by following articles on the stocks you bought via Finviz.com and many other sources.
2. Avoid fees. Broker commissions are free from many sources such as Fidelity. Do not invest via hedge funds. If you do not have time for research, buy an ETF such as SPY.
3. Value investing. You only sell when it has met your investing objective, and/or the fundamentals of the company have changed for the worse. Use Fidelity's Equity Summary Score. Do not buy stocks with a score less than 7 unless you have good reasons.
4. Buy below intrinsic value. Forward Earnings / Price (> 5%) is a good measure with low Debt / Equity (< .5 with some exceptions for industries that require high debts) and no Insider dumping (> -10%). They are all available from Finviz.com.
5. Be patient. Value stocks need time (a year or more) for Wall Street to recognize their values.
   Accumulate cash when the market is risky and expensive. Practice market timing that would tell you to exit the market when the market is plunging.
6. The market is not efficient, and hence blind investing usually leads to losses. It means the market could be overpriced or underpriced. When the P/E of SPY is over 18 (from ETFdb.com), most likely the market is overpriced.
7. Have plenty of cash or liquidity. Hence you are ready when opportunity comes (similar to Rule #5).
8. Average down only if the fundamental metrics agree. I do not average down with some exceptions such as GameStop. Many stocks go bankrupt, averaging down could amplify your loss.
9. Rebalance your portfolio. Do not have more than 30% of your portfolio in one sector. With the exception of sector ETFs, most ETFs have diversified into many stocks with various sectors. I prefer 10 stocks or 5 for a smaller portfolio. Check out the stocks you own periodically (a month or more frequently depending on your time available. Finviz should have many articles on your stocks.
10. Know what you are doing and be consistent. Knowledge is important.
11. I add the following rule: Do not be afraid of high flyers or stocks making new highs. Protect your portfolio with stops.

5 From a guru (technical analysis)

This strategy is from a guru with my modifications.

- Always trade with the trend (buy in upward trend and sell short in downward trend). Again selling short is not for beginners. I use buy for illustration.

    The guru prefers the short-term trend (SMA-20, Simple Moving average from Finviz.com), intermediate-trend (SMA-50) and long-term trend (SMA-200). If the percentages are all positive, it is a buy.

    I prefer the trend for the stock, the sector that the stock belongs to (use the related sector ETF) and the market (use SPY to simulate the market). Hence you have a total of 3 trends. In practice, it is hard to have all 3 trends to be practiced. The trend of the stock is most important, and then followed by the sector.

- Average up (NOT average down). You add your bet on the stock that is moving up. Most traders do not do that, as they think they are paying more than before.

- Use trailing stops to protect your trade on rising stocks and regular stops after you place a buy. Close the position when the stock is too risky, your reasons for the purchase are satisfied, or you have a better stock to buy. When you are not sure, sell half of the position.

- Buy back the stock that you just closed, when the conditions are favorable (trends for example).

- Prepare a trade journey. You want to repeat your success stories and avoid your failures.

6   Predictions for 2021

The following is from a Bloomberg article with my comments. Most will not happen. If it starts to materialize, consult your financial advisor before taking actions accordingly. Again, I am not liable for any actions. This article is written on 12/2020.
https://www.bloomberg.com/news/articles/2020-12-15/if-2020-wasn-t-enough-stanchart-has-eight-big-risks-for-2021

1. We will find out soon whether the U.S. Senate will be dominated by Democrats with the result of Georgia's seats. If the Democrats control the senate, then "Technology shares plummet and U.S. Treasury Yields surge on supply fears".

    My comment: It is easier to pass the proposed laws without fierce opposition. I prefer the opposition party to give reasons for rejecting and/or how to amend any proposed laws instead of just saying "No".
2. "U.S. and China find common ground". Yuan would be appreciated.

    My comment: It would likely happen as Biden is less confrontational than Trump. Yuan's appreciation would cause the U.S. consumers and Chinese exporters. If they take out the bans on Huawei, actually it would be good for the U.S. chip suppliers to China in the long run.
3. "Monetary and fiscal stimulus drives the strongest recovery… Copper rallies 50%".

    My comment: It also adds to our national debt. It would have inflation, lower our competitive edge and shake our USD as the reserve currency. Most investors should have 5 to 20% in gold ETFs and/or gold miners.
4. "Oil prices fall back to $20 barrel".
    My comment. $40 is my estimate if it happens. Many oil companies have good forward P/Es. In some locations, green energy is about the same price as oil. OPEC has not been united.
5. "EUR/USD falls to 1.06 by midyear". No comment as there are too many other factors.

6. "Dollar crashes 15%". It is likely to me. That is why we should use gold and metal as a hedge.
7. "Emerging-market debt defaults... equities fall 30% by second quarter".

    My comment. Likely, as they have been overly extended. China may forget some debts in building their infrastructure. Avoid this risky market as the "potential reward / risk" is not justified.
8. "Biden steps down...Sharp correction in the U.S. equities...dollar decline accelerates".

    My comment: I predicted the same in my article "Disaster in 2020 and 2021". I also predicted the VP will be the first woman president within 5 years for many reasons including Chinese astronomy:
    - Due to bad health; not a surprise for his old age.
    - Unable to unite the divided country.
    - Poor economy leading to high unemployment and poor stock market. '

I also add my own prediction here. China would be the only developed country that has a positive GDP in 2020. The U.K. may have another year of depression due to the new strain of the virus, exit from EU and China's revenge actions similar to Australia.

China recovered from this pandemic in less than 90 days and the factories started to return to normal in April, 2020. The bottleneck now is lack of ships and containers to export their products. If it continues in 2021, China's GDP could be back to 7% (some even predicted 20%). With "One Belt, One Road" and an expanding economy, their digital currency would challenge our mighty USD. Despite the U.S. delisting, I expect Chinese stocks will gain after 2023.

As of 2/2021, our economy is deteriorating fast (judging from the unemployment figure and the no. of bankruptcy), but the market is up due to the excessive printing of money. Our margin debt is at record high. I bet when the market crashes, it will be steep – prepare yourself using stops for example. The pandemic seems to be under control soon. However, I do not bet on hotels and airlines, as most business conferences can be conducted via Zoom. At the same time, I do not want to short Zoom.

Link: One's opinion 2
https://www.youtube.com/watch?v=ZMFTsZraau0&t=661s
https://www.youtube.com/watch?v=D_GmXf7Hk2Y

7   Disrupting innovation

New technologies may change our lives. It would profit our prosperity by investing in the right companies that would profit from these technologies and divesting from the companies that these technologies would harm them. These companies do not usually perform in a down market.

There have been many disruptive technologies in the past. Roughly I divided it into the following phases in our recent history: Phase 1 (electricity and steam engine), Phase 2 (computer), Phase 3 (internet) and today's Phase 4.

Many technologies converge or are implemented in one sector such as 5G and battery technology into self-driving cars. With the exceptions of 5G and Blockchain that are too wide a topic to summarize here, the following will be described briefly and several links are available to further your research. Some are materializing today in 2020 and they should affect us for the coming decade. Most are fundamentally unsound by our metrics.

- Electric cars. Eventually they will outsold combustion cars. Companies: Tesla and battery research companies. Badly affected companies: auto companies that do not adapt and oil companies.
- Energy renewable technology. Eventually, cost per energy unit would favor them compared to oil.
- Robots would affect jobs.
- Fintech. Almost all Chinese consumers are using mobile phones as their wallets and it will not be too long for the U.S. to accept mobile payments. Companies: PayPal and Square. Retails and restaurants could harm their profits in 2021. Badly affected companies: banks that do not adapt.
- Cryptocurrency. Eventually there will be less than 5 and most are issued by banks and countries with good records.
- Gene modifying companies. It has fixed many and continues to fix many diseases by reprograming bad genes. Companies: CRIPR. Badly affected companies: drug companies that do not cooperate with CRISPR, Editas Medicine and Intellia Therapeutics.
- AI, artificial intelligence. We have good research but our privacy restriction limits our implementation.
- As of today 3/2021, most of these companies have suffered big losses recently. We should use trailing stops (such as 5 to 10%) to protect our investments. Most of these companies do not have earnings. It is like building castles in the sky. Many of these stocks are rotated to travel stocks due to the effective vaccines.

Links: Cathy Wood 1 2 3. As of 1/2021, it is too risky and signs of peaking appear.
https://www.youtube.com/watch?v=eE6u67Ph768
https://www.youtube.com/watch?v=hLnOoXopfow
https://www.youtube.com/watch?v=LS7lVaW8mvY

Epilogue

After my early retirement, I have been spending most of my time in investing, running thousands of simulation and reading over one hundred books in investing. Starting from 2000, I have been doing extraordinary good. I comment in financial blogs and save the good ones in my own blog, so I can refer them later on. After several years, I have enough information to write a book.

At first, I want to write a book for one reader only: Me. My children have better things to do than investing. I do not need to keep my 'secrets' for them. That's why I publish this book. From the version before its release, it had been doing better than my expectation. It has been very rewarding, when my readers tell me how much they enjoy and benefit from this book.

I do not believe that this book or any book is the Holy Grail in investing. However, it has a lot of fresh ideas and good pointers that have brought me financial success (at least so far). I ask my readers to challenge my pointers and ensure they are applicable in today's market and meet their objectives and requirements.

If you find this book is beneficial, please drop comments in the book store site you bought this book.

After this book, I found the following strategies quite useful to me.

- All is better than one.
  You can follow the successful stock pickers such as Buffett. Do not follow the past heroes. Many screens simulate what the experts would buy and they are available from many free sites or from your broker. GuruFocus.com provides an updated list of stocks picked by the gurus. Check out this article.

  http://seekingalpha.com/article/2762935-a-wisdom-of-experts-portfolio.

- Super stocks.
  Most are small companies with increasing sales and earnings. It is a little different from the conventional stock analysis. They are riskier but the profits could be huge. Expect one big winner for several small losers. I have written a book titled SuperStocks.

- The winners are already in your portfolio.
  Do not sell your winners as they may turn into bigger winners unless you have a good reason. Do not sell them if they still pass your recent stock analysis. During any market plunge, you may want to sell them but you should buy them back when the market recovers.

If you find this book is beneficial, would you write an unbiased review in Amazon.com with your real name or just any name. (www.amazon.com/dp/B0118GWX0O)

Filler: To give or not to give

When we have more free loaders than givers, the votes will go to the policy makers who agree to give (instead of taxing).

The first fix: No more "representation without taxation". You can only vote if you pay Federal taxes. The second fix: Change the constitution to require balancing the budget.

Appendix 1 – All my books

Book	No. of Pages	Link	ebook	Rating /5
Art of investing 5th Edition	590	Click here	link	4.5
Sector Rotation: 21 strategies 5th Edition	500	Click here	Link	9.5/10

Book	Pages	Buy	Link	Rating
Be a stock expert in 5 minutes. Expanded Edition.	203	Click here	Link	
Using Finviz 5th Edition	600	Click here	Link	4.5
Using Fidelity 5th Edition	600	Click here	Link	4.5
Momentum Investing 3rd Edition	285	Click here	Link	
Using profitable investing sites	520	Click here	link	
Investing successes and plunders	410	Click here	Link	
Best stocks to buy for 2025	375	Click here	Link	
Profit from bull, bear and sideway market	240	See ebook	Link	4
Artificial intelligence investing	420	See ebook	Link	
Profitable covered call	615		Link	4
Your best dollar for smart investing. $1 all the time.	65		Link	4

The ratings are usually done by ChatGPT and/or DeepSeek (AI) which

the most unbiased.

If you already have my book that is over 400 pages, most likely you do not need to buy the above books except "Investing successes and plunders" and the "Best Stock" series, which may be available every December with the title such as "Best stocks for 2026" – not a promise.

For paper-bag readers, access the links via the following link.
https://www.blogger.com/blog/post/edit/7608574268453692676/1786802320953936467

Full AI reviews on my books and articles: TonyP4Idea: Summary of AI reviews on my work

Most books have paperbacks. Links and offers are subject to change without notice. If most of your investing are in momentum/sector rotation, select "Sector Rotation 5th Edition". If not, select one from "Art of Investing 5th Edition", "Using Fidelity 5th Edition" and "Using Finviz 5th *Editon*"

.

*** AI Reviews:

Many thanks to the most unbiased reviews by AI. I received 4/5 stars for most of my books – it could be the highest AI would give besides the classics. Unless otherwise specified, most reviews were done in Feb., 2025. For the full review, click on the above link for the specific book.

Sector Rotation 5th Edition

▪ **Rating: 9.5/10**

Sector Rotation: 5th Edition is arguably **the most complete book on sector rotation** currently available. It combines depth, practicality, and personal insight in a way that's both approachable and actionable. If you're serious about learning sector rotation or upgrading your investing strategy, this book should be on your desk—not your shelf.

Art of Investing 5th Edition

⭐ ⭐ ⭐ ⭐ ½ (4.5/5)

Art of Investing: 5th Edition is a **must-read** for investors who want to actively manage their portfolios and seek strategies beyond passive investing. Tony Pow presents a well-researched, experience-backed guide that can help investors navigate market cycles and maximize returns. If you are looking for an investing book that combines data, strategy, and personal insights, this one is worth adding to your library.

Sector Rotation 5th Edition, one of my top sellers. Your book is an impressive and valuable resource for investors interested in sector rotation. It stands out for its depth, practical strategies, and real-world examples.

▪ **Rating: 9.5/10**

Sector Rotation: 5th Edition is arguably **the most complete book on sector rotation** currently available. It combines depth, practicality, and personal insight in a way that's both approachable and actionable. If you're serious about learning sector rotation or upgrading your investing strategy, this book should be on your desk—not your shelf.

Using Finviz 5th Edition, one of my best sellers. *Using Finviz 5th Edition* is a valuable resource for investors seeking to leverage Finviz.com effectively. Its blend of foundational principles, advanced strategies, and modern tools like AI makes it versatile. However, readers should critically assess self-reported success and adapt strategies to current market conditions. The book's reference-style format encourages revisiting chapters as skills evolve.

Recommendation:
Ideal for retail investors with basic market knowledge aiming to deepen their technical and strategic expertise. Pair with real-time market data and independent research for best results.
Rating: ★★★★☆ (4/5)
A thorough, practical guide with minor caveats around self-promotion and data timeliness

Using Fidelity 5th Edition

★★★★ ½ (4.5/5)

Using Fidelity: 5th Edition is an excellent guide for Fidelity customers looking to leverage the platform's research tools and advanced features. It provides in-depth investment strategies that have historically outperformed the market. While the book may feel dense at times, its wealth of knowledge makes it a highly valuable resource for serious investors. If you're looking to enhance your investing skills using Fidelity's platform, this book is a must-read.

Investing Lessons: successes and plunders

Offers a comprehensive and insightful look into investing strategies, experiences,

Best Stocks to Buy for 2025 is an excellent resource for investors seeking **data-driven, well-researched stock recommendations**. Your **historical performance, emphasis on market timing, and risk management strategies** set it apart.
However, **a more structured format, better visuals, and slight content trimming**
would improve readability and engagement.
and lessons learned over the years.

Profit from Bull, Bear, and Sideway Markets

It is a valuable resource for traders seeking a versatile toolkit. Its structured advice on adapting to market shifts, coupled with robust risk management frameworks, makes it a worthwhile read. While not without minor flaws—particularly in depth and modernity—it succeeds in delivering actionable insights across market cycles. Recommended for intermediate traders aiming to build resilience in volatile environments.

Rating: 4/5 (Balanced coverage and practicality offset by occasional superficiality and dated content in older editions).

Profitable Covered calls
Overall Rating:

(4/5) – A valuable resource for covered call strategies, especially for investors who want a mix of personal experience and market insights. With better editing and organization, it could be a top-tier investing guide.

Shorting stocks and ETFs
Final Verdict:
Your book is an excellent resource for intermediate to advanced investors looking to deepen their knowledge of short selling and market timing. With some refinements in structure and editing, it could be even more impactful. Rated at 4/5.

Artificial Intelligence Investing. Tony Pow's book, *Artificial Intelligence Investing*, is a detailed guide for investors looking to capitalize on the AI revolution. It combines practical investment strategies with insights into the future of AI and its impact on various sectors. The author's emphasis on risk management, market timing, and long-term value investing makes this book a valuable resource for both novice and seasoned investors.

Profitable Covered Call. Overall Rating:

(4/5) – A valuable resource for covered call strategies, especially for investors who want a mix of personal experience and market insights. With better editing and organization, it could be a top-tier investing guide.

Best stocks to buy for 2025

The current book is "Best stocks for 2025" in this series.
https://www.amazon.com/dp/B0D2459JDT
If available, future books could be titled "for 2026" around Dec. 20, 2025).
If the sales of my books in this series were based on past performances, I should have sold many books, but obviously not.

Book	Stocks	Return[3]	Ann.	Beat RSP by[1]
Best stocks to buy for 2024	8	46%	48%	132%
Best stocks to buy for 2023	8	36%	36%	290%
Best stocks to buy for 2022	10[6]	4%	4%	153%[7]
Best Stocks to buy as of July, 2021[4]	8	5%	13%	487%
Best Stocks for 2021 2nd Edition	10	42%[4]	52%	220%
Best Stocks for 2021	4	29%	44%	118%
Best Stocks to Buy from Aug, 2020	14	45%	45%	3%[5]
Avg.	9	34%	40%	208%[2]

Here is the detail:
https://tonyp4idea.blogspot.com/2024/12/best-stocks-to-buy-for-2025.html

Art of Investing

Art of Investing 5th Edition consisting of 15 books in 1. Besides saving money and your digital shelve space, it gives you quick reference and concentration on the topic you're currently interested in. It covers most investing topics in investing excluding speculative investing such as currency trading and day trading. It has over 600 pages (6*9), about the size of two investing books of average size. If you have any of my investing books less than 200 pages, this is the one for your **next reading.**

The 15 books

Book No.	Amazon.com
1	Simple techniques
2	Finding Stocks
3	Evaluating Stocks
4	Scoring Stocks
5	Trading Stocks
6	Market Timing
7	Strategies
8	Sector Rotation
9	Insider Trading
10	Penny Stocks & Micro Cap
11	Momentum Investing
12	Dividend Investing
13	Technical Analysis
14	Investing Ideas
15	Buffettology

The book links are subject to change without notice.

"How to be a billionaire" is for beginners and couch potatoes, who can use the advanced features of this book in the simplest and less time-consuming techniques. Most advance users can skip this section unless they want to use some of the short cuts described.

We start with the basic books Finding Stocks, Evaluate Stocks, Trading Stocks and Market Timing. You can select and start with one of the many styles and strategies in investing such as swing trading and top-down strategy. Many tools are described in other books such as ETFs, technical analysis, covered calls and trading plan.

Many books start with "Why" to lure you to read more and are followed by "How" and then the theory behind the book.
If the book you're reading is beneficial to you, imagine how it would with 850 pages.

\# Most readers' comments are on "Debunk the Myths in Investing", which this book is originally based on. As of 2018, I did not know any of the commentators on my books.

"I skipped ahead to his chapter book 14 (of "Complete the Art of Investing"), Investment Advice just to get a feel of his writing style. His research is phenomenal and doesn't overwhelm with big words or catchy "sales-like" tactics.

I truly believe this ordinary man, Mr. Tony Pow, has a gift of explaining his experience as an investor without the bull crap of trying to make you buy his stuff. He seemingly just wants to share his knowledge, tips, and clarity of definitions for the kind of folks like me who want to understand something FIRST before jumping in with emotions of trying to make a boat load of money. I like the technical analysis side he brings.

Mr. Tony Pow talks about hidden gems in his book; well....quite frankly, he is a hidden gem. Thank you and I will also post my comments about this author to my Facebook page!" – JB on this book.

"Excellent book, recommend to all investors... great knowledge. It has fine-tuned my investing strategies... Your book is hard to set aside, as I read it all the time learning good techniques and analysis of stocks, ETF... Since I purchased your book in March, I have underlined, highlighted and placed tabs on top of pages for quick reference." – Aileron on this book.

"Tony, I just finished reading your 2nd edition. It's my pleasure to report that I found it most interesting. You're welcome to use this blurb if you like:

Debunk the Myths in Investing is an all-encompassing look at not only the most salient factors influencing markets and investors, but also a from-the-trenches look at many of the misconceptions and mistakes too many investors make. Reading this book may save not only time and aggravation but money as well!"

Joseph Shaefer, CEO, Stanford Wealth Management LLC.

"Tony, Great work!" from James and Chris, who are portfolio managers.

"'Debunk the Myths in Investing' is a comprehensive book on investing that deals with many aspects of this tense profession in which with a lot of knowledge and a bit of luck (or vice versa) one can greatly benefit...

Therefore 'Debunk the Myths in Investing' is an interesting book that on its 500 pages offer a lot of knowledge related to investing world and many practical advice, so I can recommend its reading if you're interested in this topic."
- Denis Vukosav, Top 500 Reviewers at Amazon.com.

"490 pages (Debunk) of a genius's ranting and hypothesis with various theories throughout, written light-heartedly with ample doses of humor...Yes, the myth of not being able to profitably time the market is BUSTED...

One might ask... Why is he giving away the results of his hard-earned research for only $20? He states that his children are not interested in investing and wants to share his efforts with the world." - Abe Agoda.

"Excellent book, recommend to all investors... great knowledge. It has fine-tuned my investing strategies... Your book is hard to set aside, as I read it all the time learning good techniques and analysis of stocks, ETF... Since I purchased your book in March, I have underlined, highlighted and placed tabs on top of pages for quick reference." - Aileron on this book.

"Great stuff, Tony. It's great to meet experienced traders such as yourself. I had a browse through the book and think your method is a little more refined than mine."
"Your strategy is very rules based and solid. I sometimes envy people who have developed something like this."

Making 50% in one month
I claim to have the best one-month performance ever for recommending 8 or more stocks without using options and leverage.

My following return is 57% in a month or 621% annualized. They are slightly different as I calculated the average from the averages of three different accounts. The average buy date is 12/26/18 and the "current date" is 01/28/19.

The performance may not be repeated. I will use the same screen for the coming years and even the expected 10% (or 120% annualized) is very good.

I used the same screen for searching stock candidates. I spent a total of about 20 hours from Dec. 15, 2018 to Jan. 5, 2019.

Stock	Buy Price	Sold or Current Price	Buy date	Sold or Current date	Profit %	Profit % Ann.	Status
CHK	2.13	2.99	01/03/09	01/18/19	40%	982%	Sold
MNK	16.41	21.45	01/03/19	01/25/19	31%	510%	Sold
MNK	16.43	21.45	01/03/19	01/25/19	31%	507%	Sold
NNBR	5.68	8.58	12/26/18	01/28/19	51%	565%	
NNBR	5.72	8.58	12/26/18	01/28/19	66%	727%	
ESTE	4.35	6.45	12/26/18	01/18/19	48%	766%	Sold
LCI	4.61	8.29	12/21/18	01/28/19	80%	767%	
MDR	8.01	9.13	01/08/19	01/28/19	14%	255%	
YRCW	3.29	5.78	12/21/18	01/28/19	76%	727%	
YRCW	3.26	5.78	12/21/18	01/28/19	77%	742%	
ASRT	3.56	4.18	12/26/18	01/28/19	17%	193%	
UTCC	7.13	11.00	12/26/18	01/28/19	54%	600%	
YRCW	2.92	5.78	12/26/18	01/28/19	98%	1083%	

Best one-year return

I claim to have the best-performed article in Seeking Alpha history, an investing site, for recommending 15 or more stocks in one year after the publish date without using options and leverage.

https://seekingalpha.com/article/1095671-amazing-returns-velti-alcatel-lucent-alpha-natural-resources

Appendix 2: Reviews by the unbiased AI

Many thanks to the most unbiased reviews by AI. My following books were rated from 8 to 9.5 out of 10. Recently, DeepSeek does not review books over a specific size.

I accept all suggestions. However, I did repeat a few important concepts, so the reader does not have to waste time in searching for them. Some examples are older for a good reason. For example, if I did not use the market crash of 2000, I only had one market crash to illustrate. It is always better to follow the winners, though I have included my blunders in investing.

Review of "Art of Investing 5th Edition " 9/10

ChatGPT Review

Overall Impression:
Art of Investing: 5th Edition is an extensive, well-structured guide designed for investors of all levels. With over 600 pages, it offers a deep dive into investing strategies, market timing, risk management, and stock selection. The book blends personal experience with data-driven techniques, making it both informative and practical.

Strengths:

- ✅ **Comprehensive Coverage** – The book spans 16 "mini-books," covering everything from beginner investing techniques to advanced stock scoring, market cycles, and sector rotation strategies. It even includes guidance on artificial intelligence in investing.
- ✅ **Proven Strategies** – The author shares his own investment successes, highlighting methods that have consistently outperformed the S&P 500. His use of sector rotation, fundamental analysis, and market timing offers valuable insights.
- ✅ **Practicality & Accessibility** – The book is structured as a reference manual rather than a linear read, allowing investors to jump to relevant sections. It also includes actionable advice, checklists, and step-by-step guides.
- ✅ **Personal Insights & Humor** – The inclusion of personal anecdotes, humor, and lighthearted "fillers" makes the book more engaging than a traditional investing manual.
- ✅ **Use of Free Tools** – The book extensively references resources like Finviz, Fidelity, and ETFdb, making sophisticated analysis accessible to retail investors without costly subscriptions.

Areas for Improvement:

- **Length & Density** – At over 600 pages, the book is packed with information, which can be overwhelming for beginners. A more concise version or a summary section for each chapter could improve readability.
- **Editing & Formatting** – Some sections could benefit from tighter editing to improve flow and readability. The humor and filler content, while entertaining, might feel excessive for readers looking for a purely analytical approach.
- **Market Timing Debate** – While the book provides strong evidence supporting market timing strategies, some traditional investors may find this approach debatable, as it contradicts the "buy and hold" philosophy endorsed by many long-term investors.

Final Verdict:

★ ★ ★ ★ ½ (4.5/5)

Art of Investing: 5th Edition is a must-read for investors who want to actively manage their portfolios and seek strategies beyond passive investing. Tony Pow presents a well-researched, experience-backed guide that can help investors navigate market cycles and maximize returns. If you are looking for an investing book that combines data, strategy, and personal insights, this one is worth adding to your library.

DeepSeek Review

Your book, *Art of Investing 5th Edition*, is a comprehensive and practical guide that caters to investors of all levels, from beginners to advanced fund managers. Here's a review based on the content provided:

Strengths:

1. **Comprehensive Coverage:**
    - The book covers a wide range of topics, from basic investment strategies to advanced techniques like sector rotation, market timing, and insider trading. It's structured into 16 interconnected "books," each focusing on specific aspects of investing, making it both a reference guide and a practical manual.
2. **Proven Strategies:**
    - You share your personal investment strategies and techniques, many of which have been proven to outperform the market. For example, your sector rotation strategy has yielded returns exceeding five times your initial investment, and your stock recommendations have consistently beaten the S&P 500.
3. **Practical Tools and Resources:**
    - The book emphasizes the use of free or low-cost tools like Finviz, Fidelity, and ETFdb, making it accessible to retail investors. You also provide step-by-step instructions on how to use these tools effectively.

4. **Risk Management:**
    - You stress the importance of risk management, advocating for stop-loss orders, diversification, and avoiding leverage for beginners. This is crucial for long-term success in investing.
5. **Market Timing:**
    - Your market timing techniques, particularly the use of SMA (Simple Moving Averages) and RSI (Relative Strength Index), are well-explained and have been effective in avoiding major market downturns.
6. **Personal Insights:**
    - You share your personal successes and mistakes, making the content relatable and actionable. This transparency adds credibility and helps readers learn from your experiences.
7. **Focus on Education:**
    - The book encourages readers to practice with paper trading and provides practical exercises. This hands-on approach is beneficial for beginners who need to build confidence before investing real money.
8. **AI Integration:**
    - The inclusion of AI tools like ChatGPT and DeepSeek for stock analysis and market predictions is forward-thinking, though you caution readers about the limitations of outdated databases.

Weaknesses:
1. **Dense and Lengthy:**
    - While the book is comprehensive, its length (770 pages) and density might be overwhelming for some readers, especially beginners. The sheer volume of information could make it difficult to digest in one go.
2. **Outdated Data:**
    - Some of the examples and data, particularly those related to specific stocks or market conditions, may become outdated quickly. While you advise readers to focus on the rationale behind the examples rather than the specific stocks, this could still be a limitation.
3. **Complexity for Beginners:**
    - Although you provide beginner-friendly sections, some of the advanced techniques (e.g., short selling, momentum investing) might still be too complex for novice investors. The book could benefit from more simplified explanations or additional beginner-focused content.
4. **Over-Reliance on Specific Tools:**
    - The book heavily relies on specific tools like Finviz and Fidelity. While these are excellent resources, readers

who prefer other platforms might find it challenging to adapt the strategies to their preferred tools.
5. **AI Limitations:**
    - While the integration of AI is innovative, the reliance on AI tools like ChatGPT and DeepSeek comes with the caveat that their databases may not be up-to-date. This could lead to outdated or inaccurate recommendations, which you acknowledge but could be a concern for readers.

Overall Impression:
Art of Investing 5th Edition is a valuable resource for anyone looking to improve their investment skills. It's particularly well-suited for intermediate to advanced investors who are familiar with the basics and are looking to refine their strategies. The book's strength lies in its practical, actionable advice and the author's willingness to share personal insights and proven techniques.

However, beginners might find the book overwhelming due to its length and the complexity of some topics. Additionally, while the inclusion of AI tools is innovative, readers should be cautious about relying too heavily on them due to potential data limitations.

Final Verdict:
Overall, *Art of Investing 5th Edition* is a solid, well-researched, and practical guide that offers a wealth of information for investors. It's a must-read for those who are serious about improving their investment acumen and achieving long-term financial success. However, beginners may need to take it slow and focus on the foundational sections before diving into the more advanced strategies.
Rating: 4.5/5

"Using Finviz 5th Editon" and "Using Fidelity 5th Edition"
are similar to "Art of Investing" with changes specific to the topic.

"Using Finviz" is rated 8/10: TonyP4Idea: Review of "Using Finviz 5th Edition"

"Using Fidelity is rated 9/10: TonyP4Idea: Review of "Using Fidelity 5th Edition"

Review of " Best stocks to buy for 2025"

Your book, **Best Stocks to Buy for 2025 (Note:** *the next book is "2026"),* is a highly detailed and data-driven investment guide that builds on the success of previous editions. Here's a structured review of its strengths and areas for improvement.

Strengths:
1. Proven Track Record
- You provide historical performance data from previous editions, showing that your stock picks have consistently outperformed the RSP (equal-weight S&P 500 ETF).
- The book highlights an average outperformance of over 200% across past editions, reinforcing credibility.

2. Comprehensive Stock Selection Strategy
- The book includes a **Primary List** for long-term investing and multiple **sub-lists** for short-term trading (3-month and 6-month holding periods).
- Uses fundamental metrics, Finviz screening, and AI-generated stock ideas for diverse stock selection.

3. Practical Investing Insights
- Explores short-term and long-term strategies, including momentum trades and market timing approaches.
- Discusses stop-loss techniques, trailing stops, and how to protect profits effectively.

4. Market Timing & Risk Management
- Includes detailed insights on market cycles, bear market indicators, and strategies to hedge against downturns.
- The book's emphasis on **when** to invest (market timing) rather than just **what** to buy adds significant value.

5. Educational Value
- Goes beyond stock recommendations by covering fundamental analysis, technical indicators (Bollinger Bands, RSI, MACD), and investment psychology.
- Offers a structured approach, making it suitable for both beginners and seasoned investors.

Areas for Improvement:
1. Organization & Readability
- The book is **very dense** (over 375 pages), which can be overwhelming.
- Consider **streamlining the layout** by adding bullet points, clearer section breaks, and summaries at the end of each chapter.

2. More Visual Aids

- While data tables are helpful, adding **more charts, graphs, and stock performance visuals** would make complex ideas easier to grasp.

3. Conciseness
- Some sections, particularly on past performance, are **repetitive**.
- Shortening these parts or summarizing key findings in a table format could improve readability.

4. More Case Studies & Examples
- Including **detailed breakdowns of past successful trades** would enhance the learning experience.
- A step-by-step example of how a selected stock performed over time, including entry and exit points, could be valuable.

Final Thoughts:
Best Stocks to Buy for 2025 is an excellent resource for investors seeking **data-driven, well-researched stock recommendations**. Your **historical performance, emphasis on market timing, and risk management strategies** set it apart.

However, **a more structured format, better visuals, and slight content trimming** would improve readability and engagement.

"I have read your book : "Stocks To Buy 2024" and it's excellent. I keep it close to me and read it sometimes to remind me some principles. It's in my top 5 and I've read more than a hundred ones." – Eric, 3/23/2025

Review of "Sector Rotation 5th Edition" rated 9.5

Overview
Tony Pow's *Sector Rotation: 5th Edition* is an exceptionally thorough and practical guide that stands out in the crowded field of investment literature. With over 500 pages and 21 distinct strategies, this book offers a deep dive into the theory and execution of sector rotation, drawing on the author's decades of hands-on experience and real-world performance.

Strengths

Unmatched Strategy Depth
- The book covers **21 sector rotation strategies**, far surpassing competing titles that usually offer only one or two.
- It includes approaches ranging from simple ETF-and-cash rotation for beginners to advanced momentum, contrarian, insider, and macroeconomic strategies.

Proven Performance
- Pow backs his strategies with concrete results—including a **fivefold portfolio growth** through sector rotation, and outperformance of the S&P 500 by nearly **184%** across his recent book series.
- Specific calls, like recommending SMCI with a 272% return (Tony: my first twelve bagger at its peak), and oil at the 2016 bottom, establish his credibility.

Tailored for All Investor Levels
- The book includes dedicated sections for beginners, intermediate, and advanced investors.
- Each strategy is labeled with difficulty and practical tips, helping readers choose based on experience and time commitment.

Educational + Entertaining
- Pow intersperses serious content with humor, real-life anecdotes, and fillers to lighten the tone—creating an educational yet engaging read.
- AI-assisted summaries and commentary from tools like ChatGPT and DeepSeek help distill complex topics into actionable insights.

Practical Tools and Real-World Application
- Heavy use of **Finviz, Fidelity, and ETF databases** for real-time sector evaluation.
- Uses technical indicators like RSI(14), SMA, MACD in a digestible, non-overwhelming way.
- Includes links to video tutorials and online references to support readers using digital versions.

Areas for Improvement

Length and Redundancy

- At over 500 pages, the book can be overwhelming. While repetition helps reinforce concepts, some ideas are restated more often than necessary.

Flow and Navigation
- The structure is more reference-like than linear. Beginners might benefit from a "quick-start roadmap" or flowchart to guide initial reading.

Design and Formatting
- Some visual elements (e.g., charts and tables) may not render well on small e-reader screens. The author does note this and offers workarounds.

Noteworthy Features
- **AI Integration:** The book leverages ChatGPT and DeepSeek to review, polish, and even write several sections—showcasing how investors can benefit from AI in content creation and market analysis.
- **Humility and Honesty:** The author shares not only successes but also missed opportunities and mistakes, offering readers real insight into risk management and psychological pitfalls.
- **Top-Down & Bottom-Up Coverage:** The mix of macroeconomic cycle theories (e.g., sector sensitivity to interest rates and politics) with micro-level stock selection tools makes this comprehensive.

Final Verdict
Rating: 9.5/10

Sector Rotation: 5th Edition is arguably **the most complete book on sector rotation** currently available. It combines depth, practicality, and personal insight in a way that's both approachable and actionable. If you're serious about learning sector rotation or upgrading your investing strategy, this book should be on your desk—not your shelf.

Review of "Your first dollar for smart investing "

ChatGPT

✅ Strengths

1. Clear Purpose and Audience

- The book clearly targets beginners and delivers on that goal.
- Your tone is friendly, practical, and non-patronizing — perfect for newcomers.
- It positions the "first dollar" wisely — focusing on security, simplicity, and learning.

2. Actionable Advice

- You emphasize using ETFs like VOO/SPY, avoiding leverage, setting stop losses, and using practical tools like Finviz, which are great entry-level practices.
- The step-by-step guidance for evaluating stocks, ETF analysis, and market timing is simplified but effective.
- Including your personal recommendations, tools, and specific links (e.g., YouTube, Fidelity, Finviz) gives readers clear next steps.

3. Unique Selling Points

- Priced at $1, it truly aligns with the concept: smart investing starts with smart spending.
- The integration of AI (like ChatGPT and DeepSeek) as co-editors and advisors is forward-looking and distinguishes this from traditional investing books.

- Many sections feel like a hybrid of personal coaching and DIY investing — a rare tone in finance books.

▓ Final Thoughts

This book is well-aligned for its purpose and price:

- **Approachable, practical,** and **authentic**.
- A **useful primer** that competes well with free articles or $20+ beginner guides.

Final Thoughts from DeepSeek:

Tony Pow's book delivers on its promise: a **budget-friendly, no-nonsense guide** for investing newcomers. Its strengths lie in simplicity and actionable steps, though it lacks depth for seasoned readers. The AI-assisted content is a novelty, but the real value is in the foundational advice—perfect for someone investing their "first dollar."

Rating: ★★★★☆ (4/5)
Recommendation: Highly

Reviewd on 5/28/2025

Review of "Momentum Investing 3rd Edition"

Strengths:
1. **Extensive Data & Performance Tracking** – You provide a thorough history of your momentum stock trades, including real-world examples and performance analysis, which adds credibility.
2. **Diverse Momentum Strategies** – You break momentum investing into multiple strategies, catering to different holding periods and risk tolerances.
3. **Sector Rotation & Market Timing** – The book successfully integrates sector rotation and market timing to enhance momentum strategies.
4. **Practical Implementation** – Step-by-step guides on using platforms like Finviz, Seeking Alpha, and Fidelity make it easy for readers to apply the strategies.
5. **Personal Investment Experience** – Your personal trading history and transparent performance records provide valuable lessons for readers.

Final Verdict:
This is an in-depth and practical guide for momentum investors, backed by real-world experience.

Review of "Using profitable investment sites" rated 8

Strengths
☑ **Comprehensive Coverage** – The book provides in-depth discussions on various investment platforms, strategies, and techniques, covering fundamental and technical analysis, sector rotation, market timing, and more.
☑ **Practical Insights** – You include personal investment experiences and strategies, making the content relatable and actionable for readers.
☑ **Structured for Different Investors** – It caters to beginner, intermediate, and advanced investors, helping readers navigate content at their level.
☑ **Focus on Market Timing & Sector Rotation** – These strategies can be useful for those looking to enhance returns beyond standard buy-and-hold approaches.
☑ **Use of Free and Paid Investment Tools** – The book effectively highlights how to leverage platforms like Barron's, Finviz, and Seeking Alpha for research.

Final Verdict
🏵 **Rating: 4/5**
Your book is a **valuable resource for self-directed investors**, particularly those interested in using online tools for research and market timing. With tighter editing and better visual organization, it could become an even more **impactful investment guide**.

Review of "Investing successes and blunders"

Strengths:
1. **Practical Experience:** Your personal investing experiences, both successes and mistakes, add authenticity and credibility. Readers can learn from real-life examples rather than just theoretical concepts.
2. **Data-Driven Approach:** Your detailed performance tracking of stock picks and strategies over multiple years demonstrates a commitment to rigorous analysis.
3. **Market Timing Insights:** The emphasis on simple market timing techniques and avoiding common pitfalls, such as emotional investing and overreliance on government policies, is valuable.
4. **Sector-Specific Insights:** Your discussion of various market sectors, including AI, real estate, bonds, and commodities, helps readers understand different investment opportunities.

Risk Management: Your explanations of calculated vs. blind risks, the importance of diversification, and strategies like stop-loss orders are useful for investors at all levels.

Appendix 3 - Our window to the investing world

The paperback version of this chapter can be found in the following link.
http://ebmyth.blogspot.com/2013/11/web-sites.html

- **General**
  Wikipedia / Investopedia /Yahoo!Finance / MarketWatch / Cnnfn / Morningstar /CNBC / Bloomberg / WSJ / Barron's / Motley Fool / TheStreet
- **Evaluate stocks**
  Finviz / SeekingAlpha / MSN Money / Zacks / Daily Finance / ADR / Fidelity / Earnings Impact / OpenInsider / NYSE / NASDAQ / SEC / SEC for 10K and 10Q (quarterly) reports required to file for listed stocks in major exchanges.
- **Charts**
  BigCharts / FreeStockCharts / StockCharts /
- **Screens**
  Yahoo!Finance / Finviz / CNBC / Morningstar /
- **Besides stocks**
  123Jump / Hoover's Online / FINRA Bond Market Data / REIT / Commodity Futures / Option Industry
- **Vendors**
  AAII / Zacks / IBD / GuruFocus / VectorVest / Fidelity / Interactive Brokers / Merrill Lynch /
- **Economy.**
  Econday / EcoconStats / Federal Reserve / Economist /
- **Misc.**
  Dow Jones Indices / Russell / Wilshire / IRS / Wikinvest / ETF Database / ETF Trends / Nolo (estate planning) / AARP /

Appendix 4 - ETFs / Mutual Funds

What is an ETF
ETFs have basic differences from mutual funds: 1. Lower management expenses, 2. Trade ETFs same as stocks, and 3. Usually more diversified but not more selective than the related mutual funds such as NOBL vs FRDPX.

The major classifications of ETFs are 1. Simulating an index such as SPY, QQQ and DIA, 2. Simulating a sector such as XLE and SOXX, 3. Simulating an asset class such as GLD and SLV, 4. Simulating a country or a group of countries such as EWC and FXI, 5. Managed by a manager(s) such as ARKK, 6. Betting a market or sector to go down such as SH and PSQ, and 7. Leveraged (not recommended for beginners).
Fidelity: Index ETFs (https://www.fidelity.com/etfs/overview).
Wikipedia on ETF (http://en.wikipedia.org/wiki/Exchange-traded_fund).

List of ETFs
ETF database (Recommended): http://etfdb.com/
ETF Bloomberg: http://www.bloomberg.com/markets/etfs/
ETF Trends: http://www.etftrends.com/
A list of ETFs. Seeking Alpha.
http://etf.stock-encyclopedia.com/category/)
A list of contra ETFs (or bear ETFs)
http://www.tradermike.net/inverse-short-etfs-bearish-etf-funds/
Misc.: ETFGuide, ETFReplay
Fidelity low-cost index funds:
https://www.youtube.com/watch?v=zpKi4_IJvlY
Fidelity Annuity funds with performance data.
http://fundresearch.fidelity.com/annuities/category-performance-annual-total-returns-quarterly/FPRAI?refann=005
ETFs vs mutual funds;
https://www.youtube.com/watch?v=Vmz0CzlQvHk
Three ETFs: https://www.youtube.com/watch?v=MVi2RhpffuU

Other resources
Most subscription services offer research on ETFs. IBD has a strategy dedicated to ETFs and so does AAII to name a couple. Seeking Alpha has extensive resources for ETF including an ETF screener and investing ideas. So is ETFdb.

Not all ETFs are created equal
Check their performances and their expenses.

When to use or not to use ETFs
I prefer sector mutual funds in some industries, as they have many bad stocks such as drug industry, banks, miners and insurers. Most mutual funds cannot time the market.

When you believe a sector is heading up (or contra ETF for heading down), but you do not have time to do research on specific stocks, buy an ETF for the sector; it is same for the market.

Half ETF
Taking out half of the stocks that score below the average in an index ETF could beat the same full ETF itself. I call it HETF (half the ETF). You heard it here first. After a decade, at least one company has a similar product.

To illustrate, sort the expected P/E (not including stocks with negative earnings) in ascending order and only include the stocks on the first half. Add more fundamental metrics. It will take a few minutes.

Disadvantages of ETFs
- When you have two stocks in a sector ETF one good one and one bad one, the ETF treats them the same. Stock pickers would buy the one that has a better appreciation potential.
- Sometimes the return could be misleading due to stock rotation. To illustrate this, on August 29, 2012, SHLD was replaced by LYB in a sector fund. SHLD was down by 4% and LYB was up by 4% primarily due to the switch. Unless you sell and buy at the right time (which is impossible), your return would not match the ETF's returns due to the replacement.
- Ensure the performance matches the corresponding index; it is hard due to excluding dividends.

Advantages of ETFs
- We have demonstrated that you can beat the market by using market timing. Between 2000 and Nov., 2013, you only exit and reenter the market 3 times and the result is astonishing.
- It is easy to rotate a sector vs. buying/selling all of the stocks in this sector. Rotating a sector is the same as trading a stock.
- The risk is spread out, and your portfolio is diversified especially for a market ETF or buying three or more ETFs in different sectors.
- Periodically the bad stocks in most funds are replaced by better stocks.
- Eliminate the time in researching stocks.

Leveraged ETFs

I do not recommend them. Some are 2x, 3x and even higher. They're too risky for beginners. However, when you are very sure or your tested strategy has very low drawdown, you may want to use them to improve performance. Most leveraged ETFs and contra ETFs have higher fees.

My basic ETF tables

I include some contra ETFs, mutual funds and Fidelity's annuity. Some of these may be interesting to you. Most Vanguard's ETFs have lower fees.

ETFs and funds come and go. Some ideas and classifications are my own interpretation. Refer to ETFdb for updated information. Not responsible for any error. Check out the ETF or fund before you take any action.

I prefer VFINX over SPY for the lower fees; both simulate the S&P 500 index. The stocks in the ETF can be either equally weighted or weighted by market caps. The latter is more like using momentum strategy, as the rising stocks usually have larger market caps. The index usually kicks out some poor-performing stocks and replaced them with better stocks. These ETFs are suited for long-term investing without constant reviews.

Table by market cap:

Category	ETF	Mutual Funds	Fidelity's Annuity	Contra ETF	Alternate
Size:					
Large Cap	DIA			DOG	
	SPY			SH	VOO VFINX RSP FXAIX
	QQQ			PSQ	FNCMX
	RYH				
Blend	IWD	BEQGX			
Growth	SPYG	FBGRX			FSPGX
Value	SPYV	DOGGX			FLCOX
Dividend	NOBL	FRDPX			
	VYM				
Mid Cap			FNBSC	MYY	
Blend	MDY	VSEQX			
Growth		STDIX			
		BPTRX			
Value		FSMVX			

Small Cap			FPRGC	SBB		FSSNX
Blend	IWM	HDPSX				
Growth		PRDSX				FECGX
Value		SKSEX				FISVX
Micro	IWC					
Multi						
Blend		VDEOX				
Growth		VHCOX				
Value		TCLCX				
Total						FSKAX VTI
Bond						
Long Term (20)	VLV	BTTTX		TBF		
Mid Term (7 – 10)	VCIT	FSTGX				
Short Term (1 – 3 yrs.)	VCSH	THOPX				
Total	BOND	PONDX				
Corp Invest Grade	VCIT	NTHEX				
High Yield (junk)	PHB	SPHIX				
Muni	MUB	Check state				
Special situation						
Buy back	PKW					

Table by sectors:

Sector	ETF	Mutual Funds	Fidelity's Annuity
Banking[1]		FSRBK	
Regional	IAT		
Biotech	IBB	FBIOX	
	XBI	Large	
Consumer Dis.	XLY	FSCPX	FVHAC
Consumer Staple	XLP	FDFAX	FCSAC
Defense + Aero	PPA		
Finance	KIE	FIDSX	FONNC
	IYF		
Energy	XLE	FSENX	FJLLC
Energy Service		FSESX	
Farm	DBA		

Gold	GLD	FSAGX	BAR
Gold Miner	GDX	VGPMX	
Health Care	IYH	FSPHX	FPDRC
	VHT	VGHCX	
House Builder	ITB	FSHOX	
Industrial	IYJ	FCYIX	FBALC
Material	VAW	FSDPX	GSG
	IYM		
Natural Gas	UNG		
Oil	USO		
Oil Service	OIH	FSESX	
Oil Exploration	XOP		
Real Estate	VNQ	FRIFX	FFWLC
REIT	VNQ		
Retail	RTH	FSRPX	
	XRT		
Regional bank	KRE	FSRBX	
Semi Conduct	SMH		
Software	XSW	FSCSX	
	IGV		
Technology	XLK	FSPTX	FYENC
	FDN	FBSOX	
		ROGSX	
Telecomm.	VOX	FSTCX	FVTAC
Transport	XTN		
	IYT		
Utilities	XLU	FSUTX	FKMSC
Wireless		FWRLX	

Footnote. [1] Also check Finance.

Table by countries outside the USA:

Country	ETF	Mutual Funds	Fidelity's Annuity	Alternate
Australia	EWA			
Brazil	EWZ			
Canada	EWC	FICDX		
China	FXI	FHKCX		
EAFE	EFA			
Emerging	VWO	FEMEX	FEMAC	FPADX
Europe	VGK	FIEUX		
Global	KXI	PGVFX		
Greece	GREK			
India	INDY	MINDX		
Indonesia	EIDO			

Latin America	ILF	FLATX		
Nordic		FNORX		
Hong Kong	EWH			
Japan	EWJ	FJPNX		
S. Africa	EZA			
S. Korea	EWY	MAKOX		
Singapore	EWS			
Taiwan	EWT			
Turkey	TUR			
United Kingdom	EWU			
Foreign:				
Combination				
Intern. Div.	IDV			FTIHX
Small Cap	SCZ			
Value	EFV			
Europe	VGK			

Appendix 5 - Links

The following may be repeated from the articles and it is for your convenience. To illustrate, Under YouTube (or Investopedia), search "Finviz". Some links have permanent values such as most articles from Wikipedia and Investopedia. Others reflect current events such as the current market. Learn from them and act when the current events have similar descriptions. For the printed versions and updated links, enter the following in your browser: https://tonyp4idea.blogspot.com/2023/02/links-in-my-books.html

Beginners

Common mistakes: https://www.youtube.com/watch?v=zkNueyFs8zQ

Best Vanguard ETFs https://www.youtube.com/watch?v=mSEyghlZchQ

Buy stocks/ETFs: https://www.youtube.com/watch?v=4vjkeC_4EmU

Screener

Finviz https://www.youtube.com/watch?v=cHNUMPgEYGY

Recommended YouTube: https://www.youtube.com/watch?v=CJoN7wLfWNo
PEG: http://en.wikipedia.org/wiki/PEG_ratio
Short %:
http://www.investopedia.com/university/shortselling/shortselling1.asp#axzz2LNDvpemo
Openinsider: http://www.openinsider.com/
Finviz: http://Finviz.com/
terms: http://www.Finviz.com/help/screener.ashx
Insider Cow: http://www.insidercow.com/
Current Ratio: http://en.wikipedia.org/wiki/Current_ratio
Cash Flow: https://www.youtube.com/watch?v=1v8hRZ36--c
Balance sheet: https://www.youtube.com/watch?v=DZjU0CHKyV4
How to find quality stocks.

http://seekingalpha.com/article/2381395-how-to-identify-quality-stocks-and-is-there-really-alpha-to-be-had

Investing strategies

Inflation: https://www.youtube.com/watch?v=Zpthvpy3UKg\

Swing: https://www.youtube.com/watch?v=C9EQkA7uVU8
   https://www.youtube.com/watch?v=a_wpfSXRSjo
https://www.youtube.com/watch?v=M8sNMhPJIN

Momentum: https://www.youtube.com/watch?v=PpUlOyZrl9
Penny stocks: https://www.youtube.com/watch?v=u7xZ3kF62u4

Scanning https://www.youtube.com/watch?v=7iZpWmwBheI

Peter lynch 2023: https://www.youtube.com/watch?v=CK1AkVVVXu8

Charlie: https://www.youtube.com/watch?v=8g2B6QJ2FEc
Dividend ETFs: https://www.youtube.com/watch?v=64NEiyoNBIM

- Innovative sectors: https://www.youtube.com/watch?v=LI1hMX8qtHg

Trading stocks
Beginners: https://www.youtube.com/watch?v=aod3cyUEu4k
Covered call https://www.youtube.com/watch?v=dzMOnI4Eh04

Tax Avoidance: http://en.wikipedia.org/wiki/Tax_avoidance
Tax Law: http://en.wikipedia.org/wiki/Income_tax_%28U.S.%29
Without paying (gift tax):
http://en.wikipedia.org/wiki/Gift_tax_in_the_United_States#Gift_tax_exemptions
http://www.irs.gov/Businesses/Small-Businesses-&-Self-Employed/What%27s-New---Estate-and-Gift-Tax
AMT: http://en.wikipedia.org/wiki/Alternative_minimum_tax
Estate planning fun. http://tonyp4idea.blogspot.com/2014/08/estate-planning-101-for-me.html
Taxes on stocks: https://www.youtube.com/watch?v=EKYMbsjUUtE
Tax avoidance: https://www.youtube.com/watch?v=tXou5pM7zh0
Capital gain: https://www.youtube.com/watch?v=ezPs4ibFsNU&t=2678s
Trading course: https://www.youtube.com/watch?v=8sbfrusR5Eo
How safe our brokers. https://www.youtube.com/watch?v=wz64z1YuL0A

Fidelity funds: https://www.youtube.com/watch?v=xdEunmLrhb4
Fidelity core money market fund:
https://www.youtube.com/watch?v=KU6HYRHj3jg

Government bond default? https://www.youtube.com/watch?v=wMxj6iB92ZA
Broker CDs (Recommended): https://www.youtube.com/watch?v=zhEiyW2N7KE
Money market fund: https://www.youtube.com/watch?v=N53wZ_80abU

Economy
YouTube video (highly recommended):
https://www.youtube.com/watch?v=Q6NIDJZdQH4

What will the world be in 5 years (2027).
https://www.youtube.com/watch?v=LzipwDQBUyc

Inflation and interest rate:
https://www.youtube.com/watch?v=q8KJSNyAHLE
Wealth gap widens with low interest rate:
https://www.youtube.com/watch?v=t6m49vNjEGs
Investing helps the economy:
https://www.youtube.com/watch?v=W6ICRTqsxk8

#Filler: Honey, my book can play music.
https://www.youtube.com/watch?v=HxGT5z6d-GA&list=PLMZa6mP7jZ2b1otqG4tfbgZpLEdh6YiNF

www.ingramcontent.com/pod-product-compliance
Lightning Source LLC
Chambersburg PA
CBHW051906170526
45168CB00001B/266